D0942064

CANAL HOUSE
COOKING

Copyright © 2013 by Christopher Hirsheimer & Melissa Hamilton
Photographs copyright © 2013 by Christopher Hirsheimer
Illustrations copyright © 2013 by Melissa Hamilton

All rights reserved. No part of this book may be reproduced or transmitted in any
manner whatsoever without written permission from the publisher, except in the
case of brief quotations embodied in critical articles or reviews.

CANAL HOUSE

No. 6 Coryell Street

Lambertville, NJ 08530

thecanalhouse.com

ISBN 978-0-9827-3948-8

Printed in China

Book design by CANAL HOUSE, a group of artists who collaborate on design projects.
This book was designed by Christopher Hirsheimer, Melissa Hamilton & Teresa Hopkins.
Edited by Margo True & Copyedited by Valerie Saint-Rossy.
The Editorial Team: Frani Beadle, Michelle Fuerst, Julia Lee & Kate Winslow.

With great appreciation to
Jay Murrie, Lex Alexander & Lori De Mori

Distributed to the trade by
Andrews McMeel Publishing, LLC
an Andrews McMeel Universal Company
1130 Walnut Street, Kansas City, Missouri 64106

www.andrewsmcmeel.com

13 14 15 16 17 18 TEN 10 9 8 7 6 5 4 3 2 1

ATTENTION: SCHOOLS AND BUSINESSES

Andrews McMeel books are available at quantity discounts with bulk purchase for
educational, business, or sales promotional use. For information, please e-mail
the Andrews McMeel Publishing Special Sales Department:

specialsales@amuniversal.com

CANAL HOUSE
COOKING

Volume Nº 8

Hirsheimer & Hamilton

Welcome to Canal House—our studio, workshop, dining room, office, kitchen, and atelier devoted to good ideas and good work relating to the world of food. We write, photograph, design, and paint, but in our hearts we both think of ourselves as cooks first.

Our loft studio is in an old red brick warehouse. A beautiful, lazy canal runs alongside the building. We have a simple galley kitchen. Two small apartment-size stoves sit snugly side by side against a white tiled wall. We have a dishwasher, but prefer to hand wash the dishes so we can look out of the tall window next to the sink and see the ducks swimming in the canal or watch the raindrops splashing into the water.

And every day we cook. Starting in the morning we tell each other what we made for dinner the night before. Midday, we stop our work, set the table simply with paper napkins, and have lunch. We cook seasonally because that's what makes sense. So it came naturally to write down what we cook. The recipes in our books are what we make for ourselves and our families all year long. If you cook your way through a few, you'll see that who we are comes right through in the pages: that we are crazy for tomatoes in summer, make braises and stews all fall, and turn oranges into marmalade in winter.

Canal House Cooking is home cooking by home cooks for home cooks. We use ingredients found in most markets. All the recipes are easy to prepare for the novice and experienced cook alike. The everyday practice of simple cooking and the enjoyment of eating are two of the greatest pleasures in life.

Christopher and Melissa currently publish *Canal House Cooking*, for which they collaborate on all aspects. They were the recipients of the 2013 James Beard Foundation Award in the General Cooking category for their cookbook, *Canal House Cooks Every Day* (Andrews McMeel, 2012). They write The Seasonal Cooks column for *Bon Appétit* magazine. Their daily blog, "Canal House Cooks Lunch", has thousands of followers. Visit them at thecanalhouse.com.

Christopher Hirsheimer is a home cook, writer, photographer, and cofounder of Canal House in Lambertville, New Jersey. Hirsheimer was one of the founders of *Saveur*, where she was executive editor. She cowrote the award-winning *Saveur Cooks* series and *The San Francisco Ferry Plaza Farmers' Market Cookbook* (Chronicle, 2006).

Melissa Hamilton is a home cook, writer, painter, and cofounder of Canal House, in Lambertville, New Jersey. She previously worked at *Martha Stewart Living* and *Cook's Illustrated*, before she joined *Saveur*, first as the test kitchen director, and then served as its food editor.

Facing page, top row: Melissa (left) and Christopher (right) in Siena; bottom: our rented farmhouse kitchen in Tuscany

Vini & The Italian Bitters

sangiovese 12, prosecco & aperol 17

italian dark & stormy 17, cynar cocktail 17

the art of eating in italy in the summertime 18

Working Up an Appetito

marinated raw eggplant 22, marinated eggplant 22

marinated sliced eggplant with thyme 23

pickled pearl onions 26

green olive, fennel & parsley salad 26, marinated zucchini 27

marinated roasted peppers 30

hard-boiled eggs & tomatoes bathed in a lemony dressing 30

salsa verde spooned on hard-boiled eggs 31, salsa verde with ground almonds 31

poached vegetables with savory zabaione 33

Pasta ▫ Pasta ▫ Pasta

lumache with zucchini & clams 36, pasta with olives, capers & lemon 37

hot spaghetti tossed with raw tomato sauce 38

pasta with sardines & fennel 40, pasta with radicchio & pancetta 40

spaghetti with cherry tomatoes 43

pasta with tuna & parsley 43, chickpeas terra e mar 44

mezzi rigatoni with tomatoes, lots of herbs, hot oil & mozzarella 47

pasta salad with shrimp & peas 48, pasta salad with broccoli rabe & salami 51

Pesci

grilled red snapper wrapped in fig leaves 54, acqua pazza 57

cold poached sea bass & lemon-anchovy maionese 58

tuna crudo with purlsane & arugula 58, grilled swordfish with tarragon sauce 61

mixed seafood grill with salmoriglio 62, harissa mussels 63

salmon carpaccio alla harry's bar 64

Big Birds & a little rabbit

chicken wrapped in prosciutto with anchovy butter 68, chicken alla diavola 69
grilled chicken involtini 70, porchetta-style chicken 71
fried rabbit & fritto misto of herbs 73

Carni

a pile of grilled lamb chops scottadito 76, lamb polpette 77
a coil of italian sausage & broccoli rabe 79, grilled veal birds 81
braised pork with romano & string beans 82, pork chops & marinated roasted peppers 85

Eat Your Verdure

avocados with lemon-supreme vinaigrette 88
cauliflower salad with green olives, radishes & parsley 88
romano beans in tomato sauce 89, string bean salad with hazelnuts & cream 89
peppers roasted with anchovies & butter 92, zucchini with spicy anchovy butter 92
tomatoes with tonnato sauce 93, tomatoes stuffed with tuna salad 95
potatoes with anchovies & red pepper flakes 95
eggplant cooked in the coals 96, eggplant with smoky tomato & harissa sauce 96
green pea & prosciutto frittata 98, zucchini pancakes 99
white beans with spicy black olive vinaigrette 100, cooking dried beans 100

Pizza ◦ Pizza ◦ Pizza

pizza dough 104, grilled pizza margherita 105, prosciutto, lemon & olive pizza 107
white clam pizza 107, potato & onion pizza 107, escarole, fontina & black olive pizza 109
pizza with harissa mussels 109, raw tomato sauce 109

Dolci

wine-poached apricots with ricotta 113, raspberry tart with mascarpone cream 114
fig gelato 117, almond milk ice cream 118, quick almond milk ice cream 118
almond cookies 119, biscotti di anice 122, zaletti 123

IT'S STRAIGHT UP TWELVE O'CLOCK, and the town's noon whistle blows just to make the point—it's lunchtime. Most days we write and photograph in the morning, stopping for lunch as it fits into our day. But today, company is coming in an hour. We quickly tidy up, clearing off our big work table in the center of the studio. We cover it with brown paper from a roll that we keep in the back and set the table with dishtowel napkins, mismatched hotel silverware, water and wine glasses, and little white dishes of Maldon salt and coarsely ground black pepper. We both put on aprons, and hustle into the kitchen.

Our workspace is narrow, just three-by-twelve feet, but we don't mind—we like cooking together. We can cook anywhere on anything. We tease each other that if left without other resources, we could use a car radiator as a stove. We are so used to sharing kitchen space and tasks that we can communicate with a nod, a look, a gesture—it's our own language developed over a long time. We pass, reach across and over each other, like two people who have danced together for many years. We know each other's steps.

This morning on the way to the studio one of us stopped at the fish market and picked up small, sweet Manila clams flown in from Puget Sound. We stashed two wet brown bags of them in the fridge. The other picked long zucchini from her garden. It's hard to keep up with zucchini, and these had been hidden under huge leaves, where they had grown far too big. But we'll find a way to use them.

"So what should we make?" we ask each other. "How about a pasta?" We remember that we have lumache, the snail-shell shape, in our pantry. It seems like a perfect fit: once removed from their hard purple-lined shells, the clams can slip inside "shells" of soft pasta. So we have a plan: we decide to add a salad, some good bread, a bottle of Sangiovese, and now we have a fine menu for our guests.

Our style of cooking has logic and order, and today the clams need to be rinsed, and we'll need a big pot of boiling water for the pasta, and what are we going to do with the zucchini?—we'd better get going.

We slide past each other in the narrow kitchen. One of us reaches up to a high shelf for two big metal bowls, puts them side by side in the kitchen sink, and fills them with cold water while the other looks for the clams in the fridge.

"Where did you stash the clams?"

"Behind the milk on the top shelf."

Overleaf, clockwise from top left: parking in Rome, sunlight in Rome, waiter in Venice, terraced vegetable gardens in Liguria, laundry in Venice, table in an Umbrian garden, grocery store in Todi, café in Palermo

"Should we salt the water?"

"What about soaking them in salty cornmeal water, so they purge themselves?"

No need, we agree. Instead, one of us plunges the clams first into one bowl of water, then lifts them out and plunges them into the other, letting the sediment settle on the bottom. The other grabs a heavy pot from the rack, puts it on the stove, and adds the clams, along with a big glug of white wine.

"This wine okay?"

"Yes, it'll add a nice brightness to the clams. Give it another slug."

The pot is covered, the heat turned to high. The clams quickly open and release their juices. We set them aside to cool.

The zucchini are next. We confer; we like to talk it over. "How should we cut them up? Or should we grate them? No, no, they'll dissolve into the sauce."

After some back and forth, we decide we want their sweet vegetal flavor and a little of their texture. So we dice the zucchini, discarding the seedy core and just using the firm, fleshy part and the flavorful green skin.

"Garlic? Onions? Yes, and yes!"

One of us grabs an onion and begins chopping.

"Don't you want a sharp knife?" the other asks.

"No, no, this knife is just fine... Well, it's so dull it's practically a butter knife. But that's okay—it still gets the job done."

We laugh. The garlic gets minced and mashed with a little coarse salt. We check the clock. It's all coming together quickly.

One of us warms the olive oil in the skillet, adds the onions, and lets them soften and sweeten. The zucchini goes in, then the garlic. The studio is beginning to smell really good. As we cook, we decide to enrich the sauce with something that will bring all the flavors together. Without exchanging a word, we know just what that will be. We push the vegetables to the side and plop a few tablespoons of tomato paste into the hot center of the skillet where it "toasts" and deepens in flavor. While it toasts, we pull the clams from their shells, saving a few for garnish. We both taste; the sauce needs salt, but we agree it's delicious.

We finish up, dividing the tasks—cooking the pasta, washing the lettuce, making the lemony vinaigrette, slicing the crusty bread. We have time to spare. So we pour ourselves two little glasses of Prosecco & Aperol. We toast. "Well done! *Cincin!*"

We hear the door downstairs squeak open and close, then footsteps on the landing. We smooth our hair, straighten our aprons, look at each other, and take deep breaths. This is going to be one heck of a *delizioso* lunch.

Christopher & Melissa

1.

2.

3.

4.

5.

6.

7.

DOUBLE
CONCENTRATED
TOMATO
PASTE

LA VALLE

CON BASILICO

PASSATA DI POMODORO

TOMATO PUREE With Basil

Gianfranco Becchina

OLIO VERDE®
Olio Extra Vergine di Oliva

Prodotto e confezionato nella
Antica Tenuta dei Principi Pignatelli
a Castelvetrano

Prodotto in Italia

500 ml℮

POMODORO PELATI • WHOLE PEELED TOMATOES • POMODORO

San
Marzano

San
Marzano

NET WEIGHT
28 OZ (1LB. 12 OZ) (794 gram)

POMODORO PELATI • WHOLE PEELED TOMATOES • POMODORO

Indispensable ingredients from the Canal House pantry: good olive oil, tomatoes, cheese, and pasta.
Facing page, clockwise from bottom left: 1. Really good Italian extra-virgin olive oil. 2. Tomato paste. 3. Passata di pomodoro.
4. Capers in vinegar. 5. Pecorino Romano. 6. Parmigiano-Reggiano. 7. Whole Italian San Marzano plum tomatoes.
Below, clockwise from bottom left: 8. Harissa. 9. Crushed red pepper flakes. 10. Olive oil-packed anchovies. 11. Rigatoni.
12. Tagliatelle casarecce. 13. Bucatini. 14. Olive oil-packed tuna. 15. Peperoncino. 16. Torcetti.

VINI & THE ITALIAN BITTERS

A map drawn by the author to keep his 5-year-old daughter occupied on a long summer day.

My life as a Sangiovese peddler began with a cocktail napkin I found crumpled in the pocket of my jeans, at the end of a trip to Tuscany. On it, in my best tipsy handwriting, I'd written, "Cheap organic Chianti for pizza!" There may have been multiple exclamation points. I'm pretty sure there was lots of underlining in heavy ink. I considered this a truly great idea. It became the credo for what was to become Piedmont Wine Imports.

I don't think you can learn about a wine—or a person—and their land and food and culture from across an ocean. The wine makers I meet and the conversations we have in fields, on farms, and at tables are my education. Late in the summer of 2011, Ben Davies (my friend and now one of my Piedmont partners) and I went to Europe in search of Sangioveses. For several weeks in Tuscany, we rented a ramshackle 18th-century palazzo near Rufina, minimally maintained by a Florentine academic and his aristocratic partner. The crumbling structure and scattered outbuildings covered a hilltop surrounded by olive trees, but there was no olive oil for us to use on the property! There was wine, though. We did our best to drain the owners' stockpile of Sangiovese in retribution for the lack of oil.

One cool morning, Ben and I headed out for a run up a rutted dirt road through the vine-covered hills, gasping past churches and Lamborghini tractors, our penance for a exuberantly bacchanalian evening. We must have looked ridiculous to the clusters of American WWOOFers—volunteers in the global WWOOF organic-farm program—and their Albanian overseers deep in legitimate toil during the waning days of harvest. As a stalling tactic while we were catching our breath during a nasty ascent, Ben said, "Tell me, why aren't we importing this wonderful wine we are drinking every night?" I had no answer besides the fact that I had never imported anything before—but why didn't we?

That night we heated the kitchen's ancient bread oven to volcanic temperatures using piles of ripped-up, gnarled old grape vines as fuel. Over wood-fired porcini and Margherita pizzas, Ben convinced me to abandon twelve successful years in the retail wine business, and our little importing company was born. We washed down the terror and excitement of new ideas with bottles of biodynamic Sangiovese from Rufina, a wine that tasted ageless and inextricably part of the land. Sangiovese is the least respected great red wine grape in Italy, probably the world. It is Italy's most widely planted red grape and is the raw material for many of the country's greatest wines, including Brunello di Montalcino, Chianti Classico Riserva, and Vino Nobile di Montepulciano. Meticulously farmed Sangiovese resonates. Across central Italy, its ancestral home, it grows with memory-making character. But it is also among the cheapest of wines, sold in bulk to large industrial bottlers. These wines are never allowed to develop. They end up muted—imposters, zombies. Their lifelessness is unsettling, speaking of sick agriculture and mechanized abuse.

The divided identity of Sangiovese is compelling. The grape is not academic or rarified: This is wine for everyone and has been for centuries. It is a fundamental component of Italian gastronomy. In Tuscany and Emilia-Romagna, it is the base of food traditions, a dominant flavor that has influenced the development of regional cooking—pretty but not frail, with suggestions of red cherry and thorns, herb, bramble, and meat. This multinote aromatic profile and appropriate levels of acidity make Sangiovese comfortable in the company of a wide range of foods. When diligently farmed, decently made, and priced affordably, these are wines for daily drinking with pizza, pasta, and panini, simply prepared foods that normal people actually eat.

The wine community can veer toward rare and cloistered bottles. I think this is a mistake, because the curiosities they fetishize most people can't find and don't drink. I care about wine that matters to people who like good food and wine but have other things going on in their lives and can't spend vital hours tracking down oddities. In much of Italy, that essential daily wine is Sangiovese, as much a mealtime staple as cheese or pasta. Back home in North Carolina, I always have at minimum a case of solid, basic Chianti in my pantry, between the bottles of olive oil and bags of cannellini beans, ready for my next pizza. For Italians, wine is inextricably connected to food, and it shouldn't be hard to speak that culinary language using our *own* larders—American, with a Tuscan accent.

Jay Murrie founded Piedmont Wine Imports in Chapel Hill, North Carolina. He has traveled the world in search of good wines and here he focuses on a favorite, Sangiovese. He is one of the smartest wine guys we know.

We asked Jay Murrie, owner of Piedmont Wine Imports, to tell us a little about the Sangiovese grape and some of his favorite wines. He chose a few from his own collection and some from fellow importers. Here are his thoughts and tasting notes.

Caparsa, "Caparsino", Chianti Classico Riserva, DOCG, Rada in Chianti, Tuscany, 2008, Piedmont Wine Imports

95% Sangiovese. Caparsino is in a league of its own. This certified organic, one-man estate makes compelling wine from old vines in the heart of Chianti Classico, with very little manipulation or modern technology. The richness and acidity of Caparsino are fundamental elements necessary for the wine to age. It's the best Sangiovese in my cellar. It is a perfect balance of wild aromatics, above average ripeness and archetypal Chianti tannin/ acid structure. It's very close to a perfect wine, and I fail to understand how anyone could not like it. Also certified organic by CCCB. Paolo Cianferoni says he makes this wine in a style "to drink a lot of." He also suggests serving it with meat and potatoes, and a little olive oil. Where did I put that bistecca alla fiorentina?

Fattoria Castellina, Chianti Montalbano, DOCG, Capria e Limite, Tuscany, 2010, Piedmont Wine Imports

100% Sangiovese. Fattoria Castellina Chianti Montalbano is certified biodynamic. It is from higher vineyards (250 meters above sea level), closer to the Mediterranean. If Rosso di Caparsa is a wilder take on Chianti Classico, this is Chianti looking at the New World. I love how open and accessible the wine is. Intense, forward, dark berry aromas, some wild herby notes, this is the wine I take to friends who love American Zinfandels and need to be gently led back to Old World wine. The high-toned high-acid thing (that I love) common in Chianti is absent from this red, making it more suited to Korean barbecue than any other Chianti I've tried.

Fattoria Corzano e Paterno, "Terre do Corzano", DOCG, San Pancrazio, Chianti, Tuscany, 2009, Piedmont Wine Imports

90% Sangiovese, 10% Canaiolo. Certified organic. This wine has real density of flavor, I feel like I have to unpack layers of earth, smoke, sage/rosemary and then, after some significant aeration, the classic Sangiovese red fruit starts to take over. The wine is so good the next day. I need to remember to age a few bottles for 5 years. They served tagliatelle when we drank Terre di Corzano at the winery in January, and it was a perfect pairing.

Fatorria Cerreto Libri, Chianti Rufina, DOCG, Pontassieve, Tuscany, 2005, Louis/Dressner ☙

90% Sangiovese, 10% Canaiolo. Is this just a sentimental favorite? We were staying at Cerreto Libri and jogging through their vineyards when Ben Davies convinced me to start a wine-importing business. When we returned to North Carolina, I bought a case of Cerreto Libri. The wine has so much personality! I think this is the kind of wine most people gravitate toward as the years pass. It is not flashy, slick, or squeaky clean, but it's alive. I like spending time with it. It tastes fully formed, and when I let myself drink what I really want (as opposed to following some wine tangent I may be on), I end up with a bottle of it in my hand.

Montevertine, "Pian Del Ciampolo", Rosso di Toscano, IGT, Radda in Chianti, Tuscany, 2010, Neal Rosenthal ☙

90% Sangiovese, 5% Canaiolo, 5% Colorino. My love for Sangiovese started with Montevertine. In my grad school days Megan (then girlfriend, now wife) and I would scrape together cash to buy a couple bottles of each vintage of the estate's top wine, "Le Pergole Torte". It totally redefined Sangiovese for me. For a span of years it was my favorite wine. Eventually, happily, I discovered Pian del Ciampolo, a "little" wine from Montevertine that sits more comfortably on the table at a pizzeria. Pian del Ciampolo is made like an estate's top wine: harvested by hand, moved in the cellar by gravity (not using pumps) and aged for up to 18 months in big Slovenian barrels before being sold. It is pretty serious: meaty, with plenty of earthy dark fruit to dig into, but you can dig in now, while Le Pergole Torte sits and gathers dust.

Montesecondo, Rosso, San Casiano, Tuscany, 2010, Louis/Dressner ☙

95% Sangiovese, 5% Canaiolo. Silvio Messana is universally loved by his Tuscan peers. Every estate owner I visit speaks of him as a kind, articulate leader, a man pointing us toward a better way to make Sangiovese. I can't believe how fresh it tastes. No leather, just berries—a light, really charming wine.

These days, all sorts of nontraditional Chianti grapes—including Merlot, Cabernet, and other non-indigenous types—as well as barrique treatments, are allowed for DOCG Chianti Classico. Today a wine made just using Sangiovese and Canaiolo grapes grown in Chianti Classico soils and vinified in the method of older Chianti traditions (tank or large Slovenian oak barrels) is deemed "atypical" and is being denied the right to use the Chianti or Chianti Classico name. This is the state of the bureaucracy's influence on the denominazioni in Italy. The idea of the DOCG's identity is being reshaped into a new market-based ideal of its "typicity" that has no bearing on the region's traditions.

PROSECCO & APEROL

The Italians are masters at distilling herbal, citrus, and vegetal flavors into intensely colorful bitters and liqueurs (and cleverly bottling them with the best labels in the business!). Balanced with a little sweetness, these odd flavors, typically low in alcohol, are used to make the classic Italian aperitifs (the Negroni and Americano are the best known of the group). Like any good herbal concoction, they aid and stimulate the appetite—just the job of an aperitif. Aperol has a bittersweet orange flavor. We like the way its bitterness balances with the slight sweetness of prosecco.

When we're getting ready to serve this cocktail, we rinse our fluted glasses and stick them straight into the freezer to get frosty cold. Pour 1½ ounces Aperol into a well-chilled flute and top it off with bone-cold prosecco. *Cincin!——makes 1*

ITALIAN DARK & STORMY

We have a fondness for making up and using nicknames. They're mostly endearing (though some can only be in repeated our own company) and they make us smile. This cocktail has one: Marcello Mastroianni. Every time we serve these, we feel like we're getting our Sophia Loren on and drinking in the good life.

Fill a short, pretty glass with ice cubes. Add 1½ ounces Ramazzotti and top it off with ginger ale. Squeeze in the juice from a fat wedge of lemon and add the lemon wedge. *Cento di questi giorni!——makes 1*

CYNAR COCKTAIL

From an American's perspective, Cynar is probably the oddest of all the Italian bitters—it's *artichoke*-based.

We drink it to our health like this: Fill a short glass with ice cubes. Rub the rim of the glass with a quartered lime. Pour 2 ounces Cynar into the glass and top it off with tonic water. Add a wide strip of lime zest. Squeeze the juice from the lime into the drink, discarding the wedge. Give the drink a quick stir. *——makes 1*

The Art of Eating in Italy in the Summertime
BY LORI DE MORI

Until I actually lived there, my imaginings about eating in Italy on a summer's day went something like this: There would be a long wooden table under an arbor with dappled sunlight filtering through bright green leaves. We would eat great bowls of pasta and pass around platters of sheep's milk cheese, cured meats, and thickly sliced country bread. We would pour wine into each other's glasses and olive oil onto tomatoes still warm from the garden, sprinkled with sea salt and basil leaves.

I was mostly right about the food and the conviviality (somehow it's as easy to cook for ten in Italy as it is to cook for one). But I had the setting all wrong. What I had forgotten to imagine was the heat: the oppressive, sticky reality of the Mediterranean sun at its most harvest-ripeningly, sea-shimmeringly powerful. Italy in August is not entirely unlike Italy in February, both have weather so fierce and at times inhospitable that at least part of the day is better spent safely indoors, withdrawn from the elements. This includes lunchtime in the summer, unless, I have discovered, you are British. For so sun-deprived are you that you will delight in taking your lunch under a blinding midday sun, preferably without a hint of shade, merrily eating and drinking while your peachy skin tans Englishly, which is to say, to a most alarming shade of red.

Italians tend to find this version of summer lunch unnecessarily arduous. The wine goes straight to one's head. Colors are all too bright, and subtle flavors are drowned out by the heat. "There are times to work on one's tan, and lunchtime is not one of them," an Italian would say.

When I first moved to Italy nearly twenty years ago, I had to reshape my habits and learn to cook and eat in stupefying heat for days on end. It didn't matter that my then husband was Italian and well versed in summer survival tactics. I was from California, where when the sun would shine too much, we simply turned on the air conditioning. But our old Tuscan farmhouse had no such modern convenience. Nor did it have screens on the windows, through which all manner of living creature came and went with temerity, including fireflies, on one terrifying occasion a pair of bats, but mostly bloodthirsty hordes of mosquitoes. I had never lived so close to the elements.

The house did, however, have working shutters, or *le persiane* as they are called in Italy. Ours were wooden and painted a dark, ashy green. And they were paragons of functionality: double-jointed contraptions that not only swung open sideways but also outwards like a visor, so we could see out but the sun couldn't see in.

Le persiane, I eventually learned, were key to summer happiness, along with the billowing mosquito nets we draped over our beds, and a daily regimen of that most wondrous of Mediterranean customs: the siesta. We did all that we could to help the house breathe out hot air and take in long slow inhalations of cool air throughout the night. The opening and closing of windows and shutters punctuated our days like church bells: opened at sunset when the day's relentless heat began to lift (though not right at dusk, which was mosquito witching hour); and closed in the earliest hours of the morning, windows first, shutters just before the sun hit them.

In summer, eating had its own rhythm too, like *le persiane*. Breakfast, never a grand affair, is even less so—coffee, toast, yogurt, and fruit at most—but delightful to eat outdoors under a fresh morning sky. By lunchtime the shuttered house becomes a refuge—a haven of cool, dim rooms where you walk barefoot over smooth terra cotta floors and make simple, delicious meals of things that don't need to be cooked: Mozzarella, tomato, and basil; prosciutto and melon; salads made from day-old bread torn into pieces with olive oil, red onion, cucumber, and, yes, more tomatoes and basil.

Postlunch, in a perfect world, you give over to the languidness of summer, go to your room, peel off your clothes, and stretch out on cool cotton sheets under the whir of a fan to read a few lines of a book before drifting off. And then, it is back out into the day. The countryside has the baked wheaty scent of cinnamon and hay, and the worst of the heat is over. You go out for an ice cream or a Campari and soda and perhaps do a bit of shopping for the next meal.

Evening is a relief, celebratory even, and summer nights are a swirl of lively meals under an inky black sky, of food cooked over wood fires, of candlelight, cicadas, and ripe peaches sliced into chilled white wine. And all the while, the windows of the house are thrown open to the night.

Lori De Mori is an American writer who specializes in the food and culture of Italy. She created the charming Towpath Cafe in London, where she lives with her English husband, photographer Jason Lowe. Whenever she can, she returns to her restored 200-year-old farmhouse in the Tuscan hills.

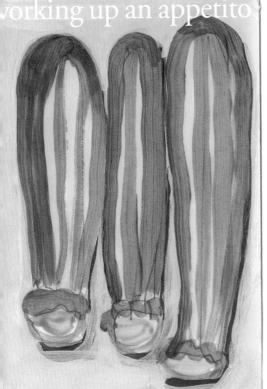

MARINATED RAW EGGPLANT
makes about 1 pint

Eggplant are often salted and left to drain for a few hours to draw out some of their liquid. In this dish, the eggplant drain a particularly long time—it both rids them of any unpleasant bitterness and begins to "cook" or preserve the eggplant. They are then well primed to soak up the vinegary marinade. Use a good mellow red wine vinegar, if you can. We spoon this piquant eggplant and its flavorful oil onto crostini, and serve them with cocktails or a glass of wine.

4 small Japanese or other small, narrow eggplants (about 1 pound)
3 tablespoons kosher salt
2–3 tablespoons red wine vinegar

4 fresh basil leaves, torn
1 large clove garlic, thinly sliced
½ teaspoon crushed red pepper flakes
Extra-virgin olive oil

Trim and peel the eggplant. Cut lengthwise into ¼-inch-thick slices, then cut each slice crosswise into ¼-inch-wide strips. Toss the eggplant with the salt in a colander. Set the colander over a bowl. Drain at room temperature for 24 hours.

Transfer the eggplant to a clean kitchen towel and squeeze dry. Discard the liquid in the bowl. Put the eggplant into a medium bowl, toss with the vinegar, and let it sit for about 1 hour to absorb the vinegar.

Add the basil, garlic, and red pepper flakes to the eggplant and toss well. Spoon the eggplant into a glass pint jar with a lid. Pour in enough olive oil to cover the eggplant, adding more if the eggplant absorbs the oil. There should be a layer of olive oil covering the eggplant. Cover the jar. Let the eggplant marinate in the refrigerator for at least 1 week and up to 2 weeks before serving.

MARINATED EGGPLANT

Eggplant, which is nearly flavorless until cooked, has the capacity to absorb big flavors. In this antipasto, the tender meaty eggplant is bright and vinegary—just the sort of dish we like to serve cold on a hot day.

Overleaf, left page, top to bottom: Marinated Raw Eggplant, Marinated Eggplant, Marinated Sliced Eggplant with Thyme; right page: Pickled Pearl Onions

Bring a medium pot of water to a boil. Meanwhile, cut 1 large eggplant into 1-inch cubes. Add the eggplant to the pot, reduce the heat to a simmer, and cook until almost tender (it should still offer a little resistance when pierced), 6–8 minutes. Drain the eggplant, then pat the pieces dry with paper towels. Stir together ¼ cup really good extra-virgin olive oil, ¼ cup red wine vinegar, 1 minced garlic clove, ½ teaspoon crumbled dried oregano, and salt and pepper to taste in a medium mixing bowl. Add the eggplant and gently stir to combine. Adjust the seasonings. Cover and refrigerate for at least 1 hour or as long as overnight before serving. —— *makes 2 cups*

MARINATED SLICED EGGPLANT WITH THYME
makes about 1 pint

We prefer using the narrow, firm-fleshed Japanese eggplant for this dish rather than the larger bulbous variety—they have fewer seeds and because they're smaller, the slices get soft throughout, rather than flabby.

4 small Japanese or other small, narrow eggplants (about 1 pound)	10 sprigs fresh thyme
	1 clove garlic, thinly sliced
⅓ cup kosher salt	Large pinch crushed red pepper flakes
2 tablespoons red wine vinegar	Extra-virgin olive oil

Cut the eggplant lengthwise into ¼-inch-thick slices. Arrange them in layers in a colander set over a bowl, sprinkling each layer with salt. Set another bowl or a plate directly on top of the eggplant and weigh it down with some heavy cans. Let the eggplant drain at room temperature for 12 hours or overnight.

Remove the eggplant from the colander, discarding the liquid in the bowl. Rinse the eggplant under cold running water and pat dry with paper towels.

Layer the eggplant slices into a medium glass or ceramic dish or a wide-mouth pint jar with a lid, sprinkling each layer with some of the vinegar, and scattering a few sprigs of thyme, slices of garlic, and some red pepper flakes between the layers. When the dish or jar is full, add enough olive oil to cover the eggplant, pressing down on the eggplant to submerge it.

Cover the dish or jar and let the eggplant marinate in the refrigerator for at least 1 day or up to 1 week before serving.

PICKLED PEARL ONIONS
makes 1½ cups or 1 pint jar

We often make a double or triple batch of these piquant beauties—
they're simple to make and last for months in the fridge. We use them
when we make ourselves a couple of icy cold Gibsons, or serve them
as a condiment with fried chicken, pork chops, or even a big fat steak.
They brighten any rich food.

10 ounces pearl onions, unpeeled
Salt
2 bay leaves

8 black peppercorns
1–2 cups red wine vinegar

Bring a medium pot of salted water to a boil over high heat. Add the onions and
cook until they are just tender, about 10 minutes. Drain the onions in a colander
or sieve. When they are cool enough to handle, use a paring knife to trim off the
root end, then slip the onions out of their skins.

Put the peeled onions into a pint jar and season with a generous pinch of salt.
Tuck the bay leaves and peppercorns into the jar and add enough vinegar to
cover the onions. Cover the jar and refrigerate for at least 24 hours before using.

GREEN OLIVE, FENNEL & PARSLEY SALAD
serves 4–6

Bright green Castelvetrano olives, from Sicily, are ideal for this salad—
they're buttery-tasting, meaty, and easy to pit. Pressing on the olives with
the side of a large knife pops the pits right out.

1 lemon
¼ cup good extra-virgin olive oil
Salt and pepper
2 fennel bulbs, trimmed and diced

1 cup green olives, pitted and torn
  in half
1 cup loosely packed parsley leaves,
  torn or coarsely chopped

Slice the ends off the lemon. Set the lemon on one of the cut ends and slice
off the rind and white pith, exposing the flesh. Working over a salad bowl,
cut along both sides of each segment to release it from its membrane, letting
it drop into the bowl.

Add the olive oil to the bowl, season with salt and pepper, and stir together, mashing the lemon segments with the back of the spoon to break them up.

Add the fennel, olives, and parsley to the bowl and toss gently. Taste and adjust the seasonings, adding more lemon juice, if you like.

MARINATED ZUCCHINI
serves 4

Every summer we plant lots of zucchini plants. One plant bears practically enough fruit to keep a small village happy for a summer, but we're growing them mainly for their flowers. We pick only the male flowers, which don't bear fruit and have long stems, to batter and fry. The female flowers are attached to baby zucchini, and we leave them on the plant until the zucchini are about four inches long. Then we harvest them, sometimes with the flower still attached. They're full of green zucchini flavor—not mild and watery the way larger, mature zucchini can be. The grocery store often sells baby zucchini, which we buy when our gardens aren't bearing any.

5 tablespoons extra-virgin olive oil
½ pound small zucchini, trimmed
    and halved lengthwise
Salt
½ clove garlic, minced

1 tablespoon red wine vinegar
Pepper
A small handful fresh basil leaves,
    thinly sliced

Heat 1 tablespoon of the olive oil in a heavy medium skillet over medium-high heat. Working in two batches, arrange the zucchini cut side down in one layer in the hot skillet and cook until browned, about 3 minutes. Use a fork to turn the zucchini over, then cook them until tender, about 2 minutes, reducing the heat if the zucchini get too dark. Transfer the zucchini to a shallow dish and sprinkle with salt. Repeat with the remaining zucchini and 1 tablespoon of olive oil.

Whisk together the garlic, vinegar, and remaining 3 tablespoons of olive oil in a small bowl. Season with salt and pepper. Pour the vinaigrette over the zucchini and add the basil. Gently toss everything together and adjust the seasonings. Let the zucchini marinate at room temperature for 1 hour before serving.

Overleaf, left page: Green Olive, Fennel & Parsley Salad; right page: Marinated Roasted Peppers

MARINATED ROASTED PEPPERS
serves 4

Pile these meaty peppers on crostini or serve with pork chops (see page 85), grilled meat, fish, or fowl. Jarred roasted red peppers can be substituted, but they won't have the same smoky flavor.

2 red bell peppers
1 clove garlic, finely minced
1 tablespoon red wine vinegar
Juice of ½ lemon
¼ cup good extra-virgin olive oil

A small handful fresh parsley leaves, chopped
1 tablespoon capers, drained
Salt and pepper

Set the peppers on top of the burner plates on top of a gas stove. Turn on the flame to medium-high heat. Or, set the peppers on a grill over hot coals. Char the skins of the peppers, turning them as they blister and blacken all over. (You can also char the peppers in a preheated 500° oven. Put the peppers on a sheet pan and roast until charred all over.) When the peppers are done, put them into a bowl and cover them to steam, which softens the fragile charred skins so they are easier to peel. When the peppers are cool, peel and rub off the blackened skin. Pull off the stems, tear the peppers into quarters, remove the cores, and scrape the seeds away from the flesh (resist the urge to rinse the seeds away. You will rinse away the smoky flavor).

Put the garlic, vinegar, and lemon juice in a wide bowl. Stir in the olive oil, parsley, and capers. Season with salt and pepper. Add the peppers and turn them to coat. Adjust the seasonings. Let the flavors meld for 1 hour at room temperature before serving. The peppers keep in the fridge for up to 3 days.

HARD-BOILED EGGS & TOMATOES
BATHED IN A LEMONY DRESSING
serves 4–6

We like the nicety of serving our sliced tomatoes *peeled*. It makes them taste more tomatoey and tender. We don't bother blanching them first to loosen the skin, we simply slice the skin off with a sharp knife.

Juice of ½ lemon

¼ cup good extra-virgin olive oil

½ cup packed basil leaves, finely chopped

1 tablespoon capers, drained

Salt and pepper

2 medium tomatoes, peeled, cored, and sliced

3 hard-boiled eggs, peeled and sliced

Stir together the lemon juice, olive oil, basil, and capers in a medium bowl. Season to taste with salt and pepper. Arrange the tomatoes on a platter, then arrange the eggs on top. Spoon the dressing over the tomatoes and eggs.

SALSA VERDE SPOONED ON HARD-BOILED EGGS

We keep hard-boiled eggs in the fridge so there's always something to eat if we're starving. But they're most flavorful when freshly cooked and eaten at room temperature or when still slightly warm.

Combine 4–6 minced anchovy filets, ¼ cup minced fresh parsley, 2 tablespoons really good extra-virgin olive oil, 1 tablespoon chopped capers, 1 teaspoon Dijon mustard, and salt and pepper in a bowl. Arrange 6 peeled, halved hard-boiled eggs on a platter. Spoon sauce on top. —— *makes 12 halves*

SALSA VERDE WITH GROUND ALMONDS

The Genovese classic, pesto, is perhaps the greatest of all the green sauces. But fresh basil is hard to find as the weather turns cold, so we make a sauce that's a cross between pesto and salsa verde. We don't mess around with machines much. We usually just mince or mash, rather than pull out the Cuisinart—it's just how we are. But please feel free to process away! We serve this sauce with roasted birds, meat, or fish, stirred into pasta, or spooned over hard-boiled eggs.

Toast ¼ cup blanched almonds in a small skillet over medium heat until golden, 3–5 minutes. Remove from the heat and let cool. Put the nuts in the bowl of a food processer and process until finely ground. Add 3 anchovy filets, 2 tablespoons drained capers, 2 garlic cloves, ¼ teaspoon crushed red pepper flakes, the leaves of 1 bunch parsley, and 2 cups arugula; process until finely chopped. Continue processing and slowly add ½ cup really good extra-virgin olive oil. Transfer to a bowl and float a few tablespoons olive oil on top to keep the salsa from turning dark. —— *makes 1½ cups*

POACHED VEGETABLES WITH SAVORY ZABAIONE
serves 4

You've likely had the classic Marsala-infused zabaione as a dessert. In this savory version, we use a pretty white wine and serve it like a sauce.

FOR THE VEGETABLES
1 large russet potato
Salt
8 baby artichokes, halved lengthwise
8 baby zucchini, trimmed
½ pound string beans, trimmed
1 bunch Swiss chard, stems only,
   cut into 3–4-inch lengths

1 fennel bulb, cut into 8 wedges
Extra-virgin olive oil

FOR THE ZABAIONE
5 large egg yolks
½ cup Soave or other white wine
Salt and pepper

For the vegetables, put the potato in a medium pot of cold salted water and gently boil over medium-high heat until tender, 30–40 minutes. Drain, peel, and slice into thick rounds. Meanwhile, pull off and discard the tough outer leaves of the artichokes. Slice off 1 inch from the top. Peel the stems. Bring a large pot of salted water to a boil. Reduce the heat to maintain a gentle boil. Poach the zucchini until just tender, 3–5 minutes. With a pair of tongs, transfer the zucchini to a tray lined with a clean dishcloth to drain and cool. Repeat the poaching process with the remaining vegetables in individual batches, transferring them as done to the cloth-lined tray, in the following order: the string beans, for 6–8 minutes; the chard for 4–5 minutes; the fennel for 6–8 minutes; and the artichokes for 8–10 minutes.

For the zabaione, choose a pot big enough to accommodate the mixing bowl you will use to beat the yolks. Fill with water to a depth of 2 inches (the bowl should not touch the water at all). Bring the water to a simmer. Put the yolks and wine in a large metal mixing bowl. Using a large balloon whisk, beat the yolks and wine together until frothy. Place the bowl over the simmering water over low heat and cook, beating constantly, until the zabaione thickens and falls into soft mounds, 1–2 minutes. Remove from the heat and whisk in salt and pepper to taste. This makes about 1¼ cups. Transfer to a serving bowl.

Arrange the vegetables on a serving platter and drizzle with olive oil. Serve the vegetables with a big dollop of the zabaione on each plate.

PASTA · PASTA · PASTA

LUMACHE WITH ZUCCHINI & CLAMS
serves 4

Lumache means "snails", so we dice the zucchini to slip nicely inside their shells. Let the zucs cook until quite soft so they meld into the briny sauce.

40 littleneck or Manila clams
    (about 2 pounds)
Salt
½ cup dry white wine
¼ cup extra-virgin olive oil, plus
    more for drizzling
1 medium onion, chopped
2 medium zucchini, diced

1 clove garlic, minced
2 tablespoons tomato paste
½ pound lumache or other shell-
    shaped pasta
½ cup finely grated parmigiano-
    reggiano
A handful of little basil leaves

Wash the clams in big bowls of cold salted water, gently lifting them from one bowl to the other, changing and swishing the water and repeating the process until it's almost clear of sediment. Drain the clams.

Add the wine and clams to a heavy pot with a lid. Cover and cook over high heat, giving the pot a shake every now and then until the clams open, about 5 minutes. Discard unopened shells. Remove from heat and set aside to cool.

Heat the olive oil in a heavy large skillet over medium heat. Add the onions and cook, stirring from time to time, until soft, 10–15 minutes. Add the zucchini and cook until tender, 5–10 minutes. Add the garlic and cook for 2–3 minutes. Push the vegetables to one side of the skillet and add the tomato paste to the cleared area. Cook the tomato paste, stirring to keep it from sticking, until it "toasts" and turns a shade or two darker, 2–3 minutes. Stir the vegetables and tomato paste together. Remove from the heat.

Pick the clam meat from the shells and add it to the skillet with the vegetables. Reserve the warm clam broth (taste it to see how salty it is) for making the sauce. Save a few clams in their shells for presentation, if you like.

Cook the pasta in a large pot of salted boiling water until just tender, 8–12 minutes. Drain, then add the pasta to the zucchini and clams. Stir in the parmigiano and about ½ cup of the reserved clam broth to make a juicy sauce. Taste and adjust the seasonings. Divide the pasta and sauce between four pasta bowls and serve warm, with an extra drizzle of olive oil and some basil leaves.

PASTA WITH OLIVES, CAPERS & LEMON
serves 2–4

We always have a jar or two of capers and boxes of pasta in our pantry (we bet you do too). We keep a tub of meaty green olives, like the Sicilian Castelvetrano, in the fridge along with both fresh and preserved lemons. (We preserve our own and encourage you to do the same. It's very simple to do, and their flavor is so much "fresher" than the jarred ones available from the store.) And on the counter we keep a couple of bottles of olive oil, not all expensive ones, but full of flavor. So a delicious pasta dish like this one, with just a few salty, bright-tasting ingredients, can quickly come together almost by itself, and at the very last minute.

½ cup green olives, pitted and coarsely chopped

1 large handful fresh parsley leaves, finely chopped

1 tablespoon capers, drained and chopped

1 clove garlic, minced

1–2 teaspoons finely chopped preserved lemon rind or 1 teaspoon finely grated lemon zest

1–2 pinches of crushed red pepper flakes

Juice of ½–1 lemon

¼ cup really good extra-virgin olive oil, plus more for drizzling

Salt and pepper

½ pound spaghetti or other dried pasta of your choice

Stir together the olives, parsley, capers, garlic, preserved lemon, red pepper flakes, lemon juice, and olive oil in a large bowl. Season with salt and pepper, and set aside.

Cook the spaghetti in a large pot of boiling salted water over high heat until just tender, 10–12 minutes. Drain the pasta, reserving some of the cooking water. Toss the pasta with the sauce, loosening the sauce with some of the reserved cooking water; the dish should be luscious and juicy. Taste the pasta and adjust the seasonings. Transfer to a serving dish or individual plates and drizzle with more olive oil.

HOT SPAGHETTI TOSSED WITH RAW TOMATO SAUCE
serves 4–6

If you have a garden full of juicy, sweet, ripe tomatoes—it's everyone's summer dream—by all means, use them for this light, fresh sauce. If not, use meaty plum tomatoes instead.

FOR THE RAW TOMATO SAUCE
1½–2 pounds ripe tomatoes, halved
1–2 cloves garlic, finely chopped
½ cup passata di pomodoro, strained tomatoes, or tomato purée
4–6 tablespoons really good extra-virgin olive oil
Salt and pepper

FOR THE PASTA
1 pound spaghetti
Really good extra-virgin olive oil
Salt and pepper
Freshly grated parmigiano-reggiano
Small handful tiny fresh basil leaves

For the raw tomato sauce, grate the cut sides of the tomatoes on the large holes of a box grater into a large bowl, discarding the skin. Repeat until there are 2 cups of loose tomato pulp. Add the garlic, passata, and oil, and season with salt and pepper. This makes about 4 cups of sauce.

For the pasta, bring a large pot of salted water to a boil over high heat. Add the spaghetti and cook, stirring occasionally, until the pasta is just tender, 10–12 minutes. Drain. Toss the pasta with the raw tomato sauce in a large bowl. Drizzle with some olive oil and season with salt and pepper. Serve with lots of parmigiano-reggiano and garnish with the basil.

PASTA WITH SARDINES & FENNEL
serves 2–4

Pasta con le sarde, a classic Sicilian recipe that is made with tiny fresh sardines, tomatoes, and wild fennel, provided the inspiration for this summery dish.

1 small bulb fennel with fronds
1 handful fresh parsley leaves, chopped
2 tablespoons dried currants
1 teaspoon ground toasted fennel seeds

2 pinches crushed red pepper flakes
Zest of ½ lemon, finely grated
1 (3-ounce) can oil-packed sardines
¼ cup good extra-virgin olive oil
Salt
½ pound perciatelli or other pasta

Pick the tender, inner fennel fronds and chop enough to measure 1 table-spoon. Finely chop the fennel bulb, and put it in a large bowl with the chopped fronds. Add the parsley, currants, ground fennel, red pepper flakes, and lemon zest. Break up the sardines with your fingers, discarding the spines, and add to the bowl. Add the olive oil, season with salt, and set aside.

Cook the pasta in a large pot of salted boiling water over high heat until just tender, 8–12 minutes. Drain, reserving some of the cooking water. Add the pasta to the sardines and fennel and toss well, loosening the sauce with some of the reserved cooking water. Serve warm.

PASTA WITH RADICCHIO & PANCETTA

Cook ½ pound torcetti or gemelli in a large pot of salted boiling water over high heat until just tender, 10–12 minutes. Meanwhile, heat 2 tablespoons ex-tra-virgin olive oil in a heavy medium pot over medium heat. Add 2–3 cloves crushed garlic and cook until fragrant and pale golden, about 2 minutes. Dis-card the garlic. Add 4 ounces diced pancetta (1 cup) and cook, stirring of-ten, until golden, about 10 minutes. Add ¼ cup white wine and simmer for 2 minutes. Chop 3 medium heads radicchio into pieces roughly the same size as the pasta and cook, stirring often, until wilted and the color fades, 3–4 min-utes. Season with salt and plenty of pepper. Drain the pasta, reserving some of the cooking water. Add the pasta to the radicchio and toss well, adding some of the reserved cooking water to loosen the sauce. Shave pecorino or parmigiano-reggiano over the pasta before serving. — *serves 2–4*

SPAGHETTI WITH CHERRY TOMATOES

Fresh tomatoes are hard to do without when their season is over. But hothouse cherry tomatoes get us through the long winter. If using summer cherry tomatoes for this dish, you won't need to add the pinch of sugar—they're sweet enough on their own.

Slice 1 pint cherry tomatoes in half and put them in a large bowl with a generous pinch of salt and sugar. Stir in ¼ cup really good extra-virgin olive oil and ½–1 teaspoon red wine vinegar. Add 2 big handfuls fresh basil leaves torn into pieces. Let the flavors meld together for 30 minutes.

Cook ½ pound spaghetti in a large pot of salted boiling water over high heat until just tender, 10–12 minutes. Drain, then toss well with the tomatoes, 1 small handful chopped fresh chives, and salt and pepper. —— *serves 2–4*

PASTA WITH TUNA & PARSLEY
serves 2–4

We're happy to open our purses and splurge on jars of Italian tuna packed in olive oil—its great texture and superior flavor make it worth it. When the hot pasta hits the "sauce" of lemony tuna and good olive oil something magical happens—the strands of spaghetti soak up the flavors, while the starch of the pasta makes everything just a bit creamy.

⅓ cup really good extra-virgin olive oil, plus more for drizzling

2 anchovy filets, chopped

One (5 to 7-ounce) can/jar tuna packed in olive oil, drained

½ cup finely chopped fresh parsley leaves

Juice of ½–1 lemon

Salt and pepper

½ pound spaghetti

Put the olive oil and anchovies into a large bowl. Smash the anchovies with a wooden spoon to dissolve them into the oil. Use your fingers to flake the tuna into the bowl, then stir in the parsley, lemon juice, and salt and pepper; set aside.

Cook the spaghetti in a large pot of boiling salted water over high heat until just tender, 10–12 minutes. Drain the pasta, reserving some of the cooking water. Toss the pasta with the sauce, loosening the sauce with some of the reserved cooking water. Adjust the seasonings. Drizzle with more oil when serving.

CHICKPEAS TERRA E MAR
serves 6–8

In Sicily, cooks sometimes use toasted bread crumbs in place of grated cheese, a holdover from harder times. We whirl slices of fresh or stale bread into crumbs in a food processor, toss them in a skillet with a little olive oil and salt and pepper, then "toast" them over medium-high heat until golden. They'll keep in a covered container for up to a week.

½ cup extra-virgin olive oil
1 clove garlic, minced
8 anchovy filets
Pinch of crushed red pepper flakes
3 tablespoons tomato paste
3–4 cups cooked chickpeas (see page 100), or two 15-ounce cans chickpeas, drained and rinsed

Salt and pepper
A big handful of chopped fresh parsley leaves
1 pound orecchiette
1 cup toasted fresh bread crumbs

Heat the olive oil in a large skillet over medium heat. Add the garlic, anchovies, red pepper flakes, and tomato paste. Cook, stirring until the anchovies melt into the oil. Add the chickpeas and stir until everything is well mixed. Season with salt and pepper. Remove the skillet from the heat and add the parsley.

Meanwhile, cook the orecchiette in a large pot of salted boiling water over high heat until just tender, about 10 minutes. Drain, reserving some of the cooking water. Return the pasta to the pot. Add the chickpeas and some of the reserved cooking water to loosen the sauce. Shake the pot gently to mix everything together. Season with salt and pepper. Garnish with the toasted bread crumbs. Serve with lemon wedges, if you like.

MEZZI RIGATONI WITH TOMATOES, LOTS OF HERBS, HOT OIL & MOZZARELLA
serves 6

Imagine it's a sunny summer day. You're hungry, so you walk out into the garden, pick ripe tomatoes off the vine, cut a big handful of parsley, mint, basil, chives, maybe some rosemary and a little thyme, then head into the kitchen to make this simple pasta dish. The tomatoes are still warm from the sun, and your hands smell of licorice, pine, and mint. It's already a heady experience and you've only just begun. When you mix them in a bowl with hot olive oil, their fragrance immediately fills the air and the tomatoes release their juices, mingling with the oily goodness in the bowl. The warm pasta goes in, along with some tender fresh mozzarella, and in no time you've satisfied your hunger in a big way. Try it sometime.

4–5 ripe tomatoes in season
(about 2 pounds)
2 cups loosely packed mixed fresh
herbs such as basil, mint, parsley,
and/or chives, chopped

¾ cup extra-virgin olive oil
½ pound mezzi rigatoni or other
short, tubular dried pasta
Salt and pepper
1 pound fresh mozzarella, diced

Using a sharp knife, peel and core the tomatoes, then cut them in half cross-wise. Gently squeeze each tomato half, then remove and discard the seeds. Dice the tomatoes into chunks that are about the same size as the pasta. Put the tomatoes and the chopped herbs into a large heatproof bowl.

Heat the oil in a medium saucepan over medium-high heat until it is hot and shimmering, but not smoking. Carefully pour the hot oil into the bowl with the tomatoes and herbs—it will sizzle and be immediately fragrant. Stir well.

Cook the pasta in a large pot of boiling salted water over high heat until just tender, about 10 minutes. Drain the pasta and add it to the tomatoes and herbs. Season with salt and pepper.

Let the pasta cool until it's just warm, then stir in the mozzarella. Adjust the seasonings before serving. It'll likely need more salt and pepper.

PASTA SALAD WITH SHRIMP & PEAS
serves 2–4

If you have an open bottle of white wine on hand, add some to the poaching liquid—it will give the shrimp a little more flavor. (Pour yourself a little glass while you're at it!)

¾ pound small or baby shrimp, peeled

¼ pound pipette or other small shell-shaped pasta

1 cup shelled fresh peas, blanched, or frozen peas, defrosted

¼ teaspoon crushed red pepper flakes

¼ cup lemon-infused olive oil or really good extra-virgin olive oil

Salt and pepper

Fill a medium pot with water and season it with a few generous pinches of salt to make it nearly as salty as seawater. Bring the water to a simmer over medium-high heat. Add the shrimp and poach them until just opaque, 1–1½ minutes. Drain and transfer the shrimp to a wide medium dish to cool (resist the urge to rinse the shrimp; it will wash away their delicate flavor).

Meanwhile, cook the pasta in a medium pot of salted boiling water over high heat until just tender, 8–12 minutes. Drain the pasta and add it to the dish with the shrimp. Add the peas, red pepper flakes, and olive oil. Season with salt and pepper. Gently stir everything together and adjust the seasonings. Serve at room temperature.

PASTA SALAD WITH BROCCOLI RABE & SALAMI
serves 4–6

We were in the studio one day, lamenting the taste of those wretched pasta salads you find in the prepared-food case—whether at a supermarket or a gourmet store. They may start out as a good idea, but after sitting in the case, they get gray and cold. Here's our version of a "deli" pasta salad that is everything you wish the one you just bought was: fresh, full of flavor, and delicious. And it's almost as easy to make as it is to buy.

1 bunch broccoli rabe, tough ends trimmed

3 tablespoons extra-virgin olive oil, plus more for drizzling

Pinch of crushed red pepper flakes

Salt

½ pound rigatoni or other short dried tubular pasta

1 cup freshly grated pecorino

2 ounces dry salami, cut into strips about the same length as the pasta

Rinse the broccoli rabe and shake off the water, but don't dry it. Chop it into 2-inch lengths. Heat 2 tablespoons of the olive oil along with the red pepper flakes in a large skillet over medium-high heat. When it's warm, add the wet broccoli rabe and season to taste with salt. Sauté, stirring often, until the broccoli rabe is tender but still bright green, about 5 minutes.

Meanwhile, cook the pasta in a large pot of boiling salted water until just tender, about 8 minutes. Drain the pasta, reserving some of the cooking water. Return the pasta to the pot. Stir in the remaining 1 tablespoon oil, the grated pecorino, and enough of the reserved cooking water to make a light, creamy sauce. Add the broccoli rabe and salami and toss gently. Adjust the seasonings. Transfer to a serving bowl and drizzle with more olive oil. Serve just warm or at room temperature.

pesci

GRILLED RED SNAPPER WRAPPED IN FIG LEAVES
serves 4

We have a fig tree on the balcony of our studio that produces a lot of leaves and hardly any fruit. We use the branches and thick leaves to protect and perfume the fish as it grills. Use fresh grape leaves if they're easier to find.

8 tablespoons salted butter, softened
6 anchovy filets, chopped
3 pinches crushed red pepper flakes
One 3-pound red snapper, butterflied and deboned by your fishmonger

Salt and pepper
Large fig or grape leaves, washed
4 sturdy fig tree branches the same length as the fish
1 lemon, halved
Really good extra-virgin olive oil

Prepare a medium-hot hardwood charcoal or gas grill. Meanwhile, soak 10 pieces of kitchen twine, each one about 8 inches long, in a bowl of water. Put the butter, anchovies, and red pepper flakes into a medium bowl and use a fork to mash everything together. The butter should be soft and spreadable.

Open up the fish like a book, flesh side facing up. Slather one-third of the anchovy butter on the fish, then season with salt and pepper. Close up the fish. Melt the remaining butter in a small saucepan over lowest heat.

Lay the wet pieces of kitchen twine out horizontally on a work surface, one piece in front of the next a few inches apart from each other. Cover the twine with a layer of the fig leaves, making a bed for the fish. Lay 2 of the branches in the center of the leaves, perpendicular to the twine. Place the fish on top of the branches. Place the remaining 2 branches on top of the fish then cover the fish with more leaves. Tie the twine around the leaves and fish making a neat, sturdy package with the leaves completely covering the fish.

Grill the fish over the hot coals until it is just cooked through, about 20 minutes, turning it over halfway through. The leaves will char as the fish cooks.

Transfer the fish to a large serving platter. Remove and discard the twine, uncover the fish (it will look rustic and messy), and discard the branches. Squeeze lemon juice over the fish and drizzle with olive oil. Serve the snapper, spooning some of the melted anchovy butter on each serving.

ACQUA PAZZA
serves 4

This classic Neapolitan fish preparation is both delicate and full of flavor. The term *acqua pazza* ("crazy water" in Italian) refers to both the dish and the poaching broth, which is stained red from tomatoes and aromatic with garlic and herbs. It's one of those satisfying dishes, like San Francisco's *cioppino*, created by fishermen who would make it on board with their catch of the day and a few other simple ingredients. We like to use black sea bass or red snapper, but any non-oily white fish will do nicely.

1 pound ripe plum tomatoes
¼ cup extra-virgin olive oil, plus more for drizzling
4 cloves garlic, thinly sliced
¼ teaspoon crushed red pepper flakes

½ cup dry white wine
3 sprigs fresh oregano
1 bunch fresh parsley
Salt and pepper
4 black sea bass or red snapper filets (about 4 ounces each)

Quarter the tomatoes lengthwise. Working over a sieve set over a bowl, scoop out the tomato seeds with your fingers. Put the tomatoes in the bowl with any of the strained juice and discard the seeds in the sieve.

Heat the olive oil in a large sauté pan over medium-low heat. Add the sliced garlic and red pepper flakes, and cook until the oil is fragrant and well-flavored yet the garlic remains pale blonde, 3–4 minutes. Add the tomatoes and their juice, the wine, oregano, half of the parsley, and 4 cups cool water. Increase the heat to high and bring to a boil. Lower the heat to medium and simmer the broth until it is slightly reduced, 15–20 minutes.

Chop the remaining parsley leaves (discarding the stems). Add the parsley, a generous pinch of salt, and some pepper to the broth. Season the fish filets with salt, then place them skin side up in the simmering broth (the fish will not be submerged). Cook until the fish is opaque, about 3 minutes. Remove the pan from the heat. Remove and discard the sprigs of oregano and parsley.

Use a fish spatula to arrange the fish flesh side up on a deep serving platter or on 4 deep plates. Taste the broth and adjust the seasonings. Spoon the tomatoes and broth over the fish and drizzle with some olive oil.

COLD POACHED SEA BASS &
LEMON-ANCHOVY MAIONESE
serves 4

When the weather turns hot and muggy and our appetites wane, we prepare this simple *in bianco* dish. The maionese alone restores our hunger for more.

FOR THE POACHED FISH
Salt
One 2-pound sea bass or other
firm, white-fleshed fish filet

FOR THE LEMON-ANCHOVY MAIONESE
6–8 anchovy filets
Grated zest and juice of 2 lemons
2 cups mayonnaise

For the poached fish, fill a deep, medium pan with water and add enough salt to make it nearly as salty as the sea. Put the fish into the water and bring to a gentle simmer over medium heat. Adjust the heat to keep the water barely bubbling.

Poach the fish until it is just opaque in the center (8–10 minutes per inch at the thickest part). Transfer the fish with a slotted spatula to a paper towel–lined plate to drain. When the fish has cooled off, cover it with plastic wrap, and refrigerate until well chilled, 2–4 hours.

For the lemon-anchovy maionese, crush the anchovies to a paste using a large mortar and pestle or finely chop them and transfer to a medium bowl. Stir in the lemon zest and juices. Add the mayonnaise, stirring until smooth. This makes about 2¼ cups. The maionese keeps in the refrigerator for up to 1 week. Serve the fish with a generous spoonful of maionese on each plate.

TUNA CRUDO WITH PURSLANE & ARUGULA

Ask your fishmonger to cut a 1-pound piece of sushi-grade tuna loin into six ¼-inch-thick pieces. Drizzle some really good extra-virgin olive oil on a platter. Arrange the tuna on the platter and drizzle with more olive oil. Stir together the juice of ½ lemon and 3 tablespoons really good extra-virgin olive oil in a salad bowl. Season to taste with salt and pepper. Add 4 generous handfuls of a mix of arugula and purslane to the dressing, and toss well. Top the tuna with the dressed greens and sprinkle everything with crunchy Maldon salt. —— *serves 6*

GRILLED SWORDFISH WITH TARRAGON SAUCE
serves 4

This unusual green sauce, thickened with fresh bread crumbs and brightened with a splash of vinegar, is also delicious spooned over smoky charcoal-grilled chicken. Make the sauce just before serving it.

1 cup fresh bread crumbs
1 tablespoon red wine vinegar
½ cup really good extra-virgin olive oil, plus more for the fish
½ bunch fresh parsley, leaves chopped

5–6 sprigs fresh tarragon, leaves chopped
Salt and pepper
1½–2 pounds swordfish steak, 1–1½ inches thick

Stir together the bread crumbs, vinegar, and 2 tablespoons water in a mortar and pestle, and set aside to soak, about 5 minutes. Pound the softened bread crumbs with the pestle until somewhat smooth. (If you don't have a mortar and pestle, use a mixing bowl and a wooden spoon.) Slowly drizzle in the olive oil, stirring and mashing the whole time to make a creamy consistency. Stir in the parsley and tarragon, and season to taste with salt and pepper. Set the sauce aside.

Prepare a medium-hot hardwood charcoal or gas grill. Rub the swordfish with olive oil and season it well with salt and pepper. Grill the swordfish until there are deep brown grill marks, about 5 minutes. Turn the fish and grill the other side until it is just cooked through, about 5 minutes.

Transfer the swordfish to a cutting board and cut into 4–8 pieces. Arrange the swordfish on a serving platter, drizzle with olive oil, and garnish with tarragon sprigs, if you like. Serve with the tarragon sauce on the side.

MIXED SEAFOOD GRILL WITH SALMORIGLIO
serves 4–8

We fancy octopus for its sweet, tender flesh. Most octopus sold in the United States is cleaned and frozen—a good thing, because freezing helps tenderize it. Cooking it in gently simmering water keeps it from becoming tough. Finishing it on the grill adds the smoky flavor of summer.

FOR THE MIXED GRILL
1 cup white wine vinegar
One octopus, 5–6 pounds, cleaned
12–16 large unpeeled shrimp
6 large squid, cleaned
Extra-virgin olive oil
Salt
2 pinches crushed red pepper flakes
2–3 lemons, halved

FOR THE SALMORIGLIO
Juice of 2 lemons
1–2 cloves garlic, minced
Small handful fresh oregano leaves, chopped
Small handful fresh parsley leaves, chopped
1 cup extra-virgin olive oil
Salt and pepper

For the mixed grill, bring a large pot of water to a boil over high heat. Add the vinegar and octopus and reduce the heat to low. Cover and very gently simmer until the octopus is tender, 1–1½ hours. Drain and set aside until cool enough to handle. Cut off the head and cut out the hard "beak" in the center of the tentacles, leaving the rest of the octopus intact. Peel off the skin, if you like. Put the octopus into a large dish along with the shrimp and squid. Drizzle with olive oil and season with salt and red pepper flakes.

For the salmoriglio, put the lemon juice, garlic, oregano, and parsley into a medium bowl. Stir in the olive oil. Season with salt and pepper.

Prepare a hot to medium-hot fire to one side of a charcoal or gas grill. Grill the octopus, shrimp, and squid over the hotter section of coals until well marked and slightly charred in places, about 5 minutes. Move the seafood to a cooler spot on the grill if there are flare-ups. The squid should be opaque, the shrimp just cooked through, and the octopus just needs a little color and smoke. Arrange the seafood and lemons on a large serving platter. Serve the salmoriglio in a bowl to spoon over the seafood.

HARISSA MUSSELS
serves 4–6

Harissa, the Tunisian red chile paste, adds rich flavor and heat to these juicy mussels. We serve them any number of ways: spooned over garlicky toast for lunch, over crostini for hors d'oeuvres, stirred into warm spaghetti or orecchiette, or as one of our favorite toppings for our homemade pizza (see page 109).

3 pounds mussels, scrubbed and debearded

½ cup dry white wine

2 tablespoons extra-virgin olive oil, plus more for drizzling

1 small onion, finely chopped

2 cloves garlic, mashed to a paste with a pinch of salt

2 teaspoons tomato paste

1 teaspoon harissa

Salt and pepper

Small handful fresh parsley leaves, finely chopped

4–6 slices toasted country bread, rubbed with a raw garlic clove

Put the mussels and wine in a heavy large pot and cover with a tight-fitting lid. Steam the mussels over high heat, vigorously shaking the pot over the heat a few times, until they open, 5–10 minutes. Remove the pot from the heat, uncover, and let the mussels cool slightly. Pluck the mussels from their shells, discarding the shells and any mussels that don't open. Set the mussels aside. Save the mussel broth for another use, if you like.

Meanwhile, heat the olive oil in a heavy medium skillet over medium-low heat. Add the onions and cook, stirring occasionally, until very soft and translucent, 10–15 minutes. Add the garlic and cook until fragrant, about 2 minutes. Increase the heat to medium. Push the onions and garlic to the sides of the skillet and add the tomato paste and harissa to the center. Cook, stirring, until the pastes are toasted and a shade darker, about 3 minutes. Stir everything together. Reduce the heat to low. Season lightly with salt and pepper.

Remove the skillet from the heat and stir in the mussels and parsley. Adjust the seasonings. Divide the toasts between 4–6 plates and spoon the mussels over the toasts. Drizzle with olive oil.

SALMON CARPACCIO ALLA HARRY'S BAR
serves 4–6

This recipe was inspired by one served at the famed Harry's Bar in Venice, where they make it with thinly sliced raw beef. Here, we make it instead with raw wild Pacific salmon. Freezing well-wrapped salmon for a couple of hours firms up the flesh and makes slicing easier.

FOR THE MAIONESE SAUCE
1 large egg yolk
Salt
Juice of ½ lemon
½ cup canola oil
½ cup extra-virgin olive oil
2 teaspoons Worcestershire sauce

3–5 tablespoons milk
Pepper
1 tablespoon fresh tarragon leaves, finely chopped

FOR THE SALMON
1 pound center-cut salmon filet, skin and pinbones removed

For the maionese sauce, whisk together the egg yolk, a pinch of salt, and half of the lemon juice in a medium bowl. Combine both the oils in a measuring cup with a spout. Whisking constantly, add the oil to the yolk about 1 teaspoon at a time. The sauce will thicken and emulsify. After you've added about ¼ cup of the oil, you can begin to slowly drizzle in the remaining oil as you continue to whisk, until you have a thick, glossy sauce. Add more of the remaining lemon juice, if you like. Add the Worcestershire sauce. Stir in enough of the milk to thin the sauce. Season with salt and pepper. Transfer to a covered container and refrigerate until ready to use. The sauce will keep for up to 1 week in the refrigerator. Mix in the tarragon just before serving.

For the salmon, use a long-blade knife to cut the salmon across the grain into very thin slices. Evenly divide the sliced salmon between 4–6 dinner plates, arranging the slices in a mosaic pattern. Place pieces of plastic wrap over the salmon, and using a flat meat-pounder or even a metal measuring cup with a flat bottom, press down on the plastic, until the salmon spreads out and covers the whole plate. Repeat with all the plates of salmon. You can stack the plates and refrigerate them until you are ready to sauce and serve them.

Remove and discard the plastic wrap. Thin the maionese with a little milk if it's too thick. Drizzle it over the salmon, à la Jackson Pollock. Serve cold.

Big Birds & a little rabbit

CHICKEN WRAPPED IN PROSCIUTTO
WITH ANCHOVY BUTTER
serves 4–6

If you've followed our cooking, you'll know how crazy we are for anchovy butter. It has everything going for it: Buttery richness, a complex saltiness, and a hit of lemon juice to cut through it all. This chicken dish is bathed in the butter and has plenty extra for sopping up with hunks of lightly toasted bread. Sometimes, instead of using a whole cut-up chicken, we use breasts or thighs. We even serve it as an hors d'oeuvre, wrapping bite-size pieces of chicken breast in prosciutto, then serving them on skewers with a cube of crusty bread on the end.

12 tablespoons (1½ sticks) salted butter

8 anchovy filets, chopped

2 sprigs fresh sage or 1 sprig fresh rosemary, lightly crushed

1 chicken, 3–4 pounds, cut into 10 pieces

Pepper

10–12 thin slices prosciutto

2 lemons, halved

Preheat the oven to 400°. Put the butter, anchovies, and sage in a small saucepan over medium-low heat. As the butter melts, mash the anchovies with the back of a wooden spoon so they dissolve into the butter. When the butter is melted and bubbling, remove it from the heat.

Season the chicken lightly with pepper, then wrap each piece with a slice of prosciutto. Working over a roasting pan to catch any drips, brush the anchovy butter on the chicken, coating it completely, then arrange the pieces in the pan. Roast the chicken, basting it a few times as it cooks, until the juices run clear when pierced, 20–30 minutes. (Check the breast pieces first, they will be done before the thighs and drumsticks.)

Transfer the chicken to a serving platter. Stir the remaining anchovy butter into the pan juices that have collected in the bottom of the roasting pan, scraping up any browned bits. Squeeze in the juice of half a lemon. Spoon the pan juices over the chicken. Garnish with the remaining lemons. Serve with thick slices of lightly toasted country bread, if you like.

Preceding pages, left: Chicken Wrapped in Proscuitto with Anchovy Butter; right: Chicken alla Diavola

CHICKEN ALLA DIAVOLA
serves 4–6

Neither one of us particularly likes very spicy hot food. The intensity of the heat can get in the way of the flavor, and we're usually more interested in flavor rather than sensation. But there are exceptions. This Italian classic— devilishly spicy grilled chicken—is one: It makes our lips burn and tingle, but the heat and flavor are balanced just right. It's the kind of food we crave when the weather gets hot. We wash it down with cold *rosato*. Bliss.

1 chicken, 3–4 pounds
2 teaspoons freshly ground
  black pepper
1–2 teaspoons crushed red
  pepper flakes

Salt
¼ cup fresh lemon juice
  (1–2 lemons)
½ cup extra-virgin olive oil

Using a pair of kitchen shears, cut out the backbone of the chicken (save it for making stock, if you like). Rinse the bird and pat it dry with paper towels. Spread the chicken out skin side up so it lays flat. Tuck the wing tips neatly behind the wings or snip them off. Season the chicken all over with the black pepper, red pepper flakes, and salt, rubbing the seasonings into the skin until it is well coated. Put the chicken skin side up in a large dish. Combine the lemon juice and olive oil in a small bowl and pour it over the bird. Let the chicken marinate at room temperature for 1 hour, turning it over halfway through.

Prepare a medium-hot fire to one side of a charcoal grill. If using a gas grill, fire up the "back burner" to medium-hot heat. Grill the chicken skin side down in the center of the grill until well marked and slightly charred in places, about 20 minutes. Baste the chicken often with the leftover marinade, taking care not to drip too much oil onto the coals to avoid flare-ups. Move the chicken to a cooler spot on the grill if there are flare-ups and the chicken begins to burn. Turn the chicken and grill the other side until the thigh juices run clear when pierced, about 20 minutes.

Transfer the chicken to a cutting board and let it rest for about 10 minutes before cutting it up and serving.

GRILLED CHICKEN INVOLTINI
serves 4–6

These *involtini* (stuffed rolls) take a little time to fill and roll up (that's the fun part of making these to us), but once they're skewered, they cook very quickly.

½ cup pitted green olives in brine, drained and finely chopped

6 anchovy filets, finely chopped

1 large handful parsley leaves, finely chopped

3 tablespoons extra-virgin olive oil, plus more for drizzling

1½ pounds chicken cutlets, about 12

Salt and pepper

4–6 lemon wedges

Stir together the olives, anchovies, parsley, and olive oil in a small bowl. This makes ¾ cup of filling. Set aside. Soak 8–12 wooden skewers in a pan of water to keep them from singeing on the grill.

Use the smooth side of a meat pounder on a sturdy work surface and lightly pound each chicken cutlet into a roughly 4 × 6-inch rectangle. Lightly season the cutlets with salt and pepper. Working with one cutlet at a time, spread about 1 tablespoon of the olive filling evenly over the meat. Starting with a narrow side, roll up the cutlet like a jelly roll. Repeat with the remaining cutlets and filling until there are 12 involtini.

Thread up to 3 chicken involtini onto 2 parallel wooden skewers. Set them about 1 inch apart, leaving an inch or two between each involtini. (Doubling up on the skewers prevents the involtini from swiveling on the skewers. See the photograph on page 80.) Drizzle the involtini with olive oil and season with salt and pepper.

Prepare a medium-hot charcoal or gas grill. Grill the chicken skewers until well marked and lightly browned on both sides, 1–1½ minutes per side. Transfer the chicken skewers to a serving platter as done. Drizzle with olive oil and season with a little salt. Serve warm with lemon wedges.

VARIATION: We also like to fill the chicken involtini with this mash: 6 minced anchovy filets, 1–2 minced cloves garlic, 1 bunch chopped fresh parsley, ¼ cup grated parmigiano-reggiano, and ¼ cup extra-virgin olive oil.

PORCHETTA-STYLE CHICKEN
serves 4

The traditional herbs used in porchetta, the deservedly famous pork roast from the Lazio region of Italy, are wild fennel, rosemary, and garlic—big, bold flavors that we think also go well with chicken. Spatchcocking the bird (cutting out the backbone and opening up the chicken so it lays flat) allows more room for stuffing seasonings under the skin, helps the chicken cook more evenly, and makes carving the bird a breeze.

1–2 teaspoons fennel seeds,
  lightly toasted
1 clove garlic, chopped
1 large sprig fresh rosemary,
  leaves chopped
1 large sprig fresh sage, leaves
  chopped

Salt and pepper
Finely grated zest of 2 lemons
1 chicken, 3–4 pounds
1 tablespoon extra-virgin olive oil

Crush the toasted fennel seeds with a mortar and pestle. Add the garlic, rosemary, sage, and a generous pinch of salt and pepper, and crush to a paste. Stir in the lemon zest and set the paste aside.

Using a pair of kitchen shears, cut out the backbone of the chicken (save it for making stock, if you like). Rinse the bird and pat it dry with paper towels. Spread the chicken out skin side up so it lays flat. Tuck the wing tips neatly behind the wings or snip them off. Use your fingers to loosen the skin from the breast and thighs, taking care not to tear the skin. Rub the herb paste under the skin all over the flesh. Season the bird all over with salt and set aside at room temperature for 1–2 hours. Or, cover with plastic wrap and refrigerate overnight.

Preheat the oven to 450°. Set the chicken skin side up on a wire rack set in a roasting pan and rub all over with olive oil. Add 1 cup water to the pan. Roast the chicken until golden brown and the thigh juices run clear when pierced, 40–45 minutes. Remove the chicken from the oven and let it rest for about 10 minutes before cutting up and serving.

FRIED RABBIT & FRITTO MISTO OF HERBS
serves 4

We are lucky enough to have a young couple nearby who raise livestock, including rabbit, in the old-fashioned humane way. Yes, it's the delicate white meat many Americans are squeamish about, but it sure is tasty. In summer, we serve it fried—hot or cold, as you would fried chicken—alongside a fritto misto of the herbs rabbits like to eat, as a way of honoring the animal.

FOR THE FRITTO MISTO
½ cup all-purpose flour
¼ teaspoon salt
½–1 cup white wine
Canola oil
2 handfuls each fresh sage leaves
   and parsley sprigs

FOR THE RABBIT
2 cups all-purpose flour
3 eggs
Olive oil
1 cleaned rabbit, cut into 12 pieces
Salt and pepper
Capers, drained
1–2 lemons, quartered

For the fritto misto, whisk the flour and salt together in a medium bowl. Add the wine, whisking until the batter is smooth. Let it rest for 30 minutes.

For the rabbit, put the flour in a dish, beat the eggs in another dish, and set aside. Add enough oil to a large heavy skillet to reach a depth of ½ inch. Heat over medium heat until hot or until it reaches 350° on a candy thermometer.

Meanwhile, season the rabbit with salt and pepper and dredge each piece in flour, dip in egg, then dredge in flour, shaking off excess. Working in batches, fry the rabbit until golden brown all over, about 10 minutes. Transfer the rabbit to a wire rack set over paper towels to drain. Season with salt.

To fry the herbs, add enough canola oil to a heavy, deep pot to reach a depth of 2 inches. Heat the oil over medium heat until hot or until it reaches 350° on a candy thermometer. Give the batter a quick whisk.

Dip 1 sage leaf or parsley sprig at a time in the batter and carefully lower it into the hot oil. Fry herbs in small batches until golden and crisp, about 1 minute. Drain on the wire rack. Season with salt. Serve the rabbit and herbs scattered with capers and garnished with lemon.

carni

A PILE OF GRILLED LAMB CHOPS SCOTTADITO
serves 4–6

Scottadito is loosely translated as "fingers-blistering hot" and alludes to the fact that no one can wait for them to cool before eating. So we dispense with a knife and fork as they do in Rome, pick them up, and nibble away. We sometimes serve these as a first course. They're a real icebreaker. It's hard to be reticent when you're licking your fingers!

Harissa offers mild heat, so use an amount that suits your taste in the paste that seasons these. It's the combination of the harissa and the chops hot off the grill that makes these *scottadito*!

2 cloves garlic, minced to a paste
2–4 tablespoons harissa
½ cup extra-virgin olive oil
Juice of 1 lemon

Two 8-rib racks of lamb, frenched
Salt and pepper
2 lemons, quartered

Mix together the garlic, harissa, olive oil, and lemon juice in a small bowl.

Cut each rack in half, into 4-rib pieces. (This way the lamb will be easier to cook and everyone can have one or two crispy "end chops".) Arrange the chops in a large pan and brush with some of the harissa sauce. Cover with plastic wrap and set aside for about an hour, or refrigerate for about 4 hours.

Prepare a medium-hot fire to one side of a charcoal grill. If using a gas grill, fire up the "back burner" to medium-hot heat. Grill the lamb in the center of the grill, moving it to a cooler spot if there are flare-ups. Turn the pieces as a brown crust develops. When the meat is browned all over, move it to the coolest spot on the grill to finish cooking, turning it occasionally, until the internal temperature reaches 125° for medium-rare. The grilling time will vary depending on your grill and the heat. Transfer the lamb to a cutting board, loosely cover with foil, and allow it to rest briefly.

Cut the ribs into individual chops, pile them on a big platter, and season with salt and pepper. Serve with any remaining harissa sauce and lemon wedges, and let everyone eat them with their fingers.

Preceding pages: A Pile of Grilled Lamb Chops Scottadito

LAMB POLPETTE
makes about 4 dozen little meatballs

Saffron, cinnamon, and red pepper flakes give these little meatballs a distinctive warmth. The currants add sweetness. Serve them hot or make them ahead and serve at room temperature—they're delicious either way.

2 pinches of saffron threads

2 tablespoons olive oil

1 small onion, minced

⅓ cup dried currants, chopped

1½ pounds ground lamb

1 handful chopped fresh parsley

2 small cloves garlic, minced

½ teaspoon ground cinnamon

1½ teaspoons salt

Big pinch of crushed red pepper flakes

Pepper

3 large eggs

2 tablespoons flour

2–3 cups panko, finely crushed

Vegetable oil for frying

Lightly toast the saffron in a small skillet over medium-low heat until it turns a shade darker, about 30 seconds. Crush the saffron to a powder with a mortar and pestle. Dissolve the saffron in 2 tablespoons warm water and set aside.

Heat the olive oil and onions together in a small skillet over medium heat and cook until they begin to soften, 3–5 minutes. Add the saffron water and cook until the onions are soft, 3–5 minutes. Add the currants. Set aside to cool.

Put the lamb, parsley, garlic, cinnamon, salt, red pepper flakes, a big pinch of black pepper, and the cooled onions in a large mixing bowl. Gently mix everything together, taking care not to overhandle the meat. Shape the meat into 1-inch meatballs, arranging them in a single layer on a baking sheet. You can do this a few hours ahead, cover them with plastic wrap, and refrigerate until you are ready to cook them.

Beat the eggs with the flour in a wide bowl until smooth. Put the panko in another wide bowl. Dip the meatballs in the egg, then roll them in the panko.

Pour the vegetable oil into a heavy medium skillet to a depth of ½ inch and heat over medium-high heat until hot. Fry the meatballs in batches, turning them so they cook evenly, until golden brown all over, about 5 minutes. Transfer to a rack set over paper towels to drain. Serve hot or at room temperature.

A COIL OF ITALIAN SAUSAGE & BROCCOLI RABE
serves 4–6

Faicco's is an Italian butcher shop in New York City that specializes in all things pork. Their display case has more appeal than the windows at Bergdorf Goodman. We can never resist buying their sausage coils when we visit; the narrow casings make the prettiest spirals. If you can't find coils, just buy your favorite Italian sausages.

FOR THE SAUSAGE
1 coil Italian sausage, 1½–2 pounds
2 tablespoons olive oil

FOR THE BROCCOLI RABE
1 bunch broccoli rabe

¼ cup extra-virgin olive oil, plus more for drizzling
1 clove garlic, thinly sliced
¼–½ teaspoon crushed red pepper flakes
Salt

For the sausage, prick the sausage in a few places with a sharp knife to keep the casing from splitting as it cooks. Heat the olive oil in a heavy large skillet over medium heat. Add the sausage and ¼ cup water. Cover and cook until the sausage begins to brown on the bottom, about 15 minutes.

Carefully turn the sausage over and add a splash or two of water if the skillet is dry. Cover and continue cooking until the sausage begins to brown on the bottom, about 10 minutes. Uncover and cook until the water evaporates, the sausage is well browned, and the center is cooked through, 5–10 minutes. (The sausage will brown quickly once the water evaporates. As the skin browns, loosen the center of the coil to be sure the center cooks through.)

For the broccoli rabe, trim off the thick stems, rinse the broccoli rabe, shake off the water, but don't dry it. Put the olive oil, garlic, and red pepper flakes in a large skillet and heat over medium heat until just fragrant, 1–2 minutes. Add the broccoli rabe, a generous pinch of salt, and ¼ cup water. Cover and cook, turning it as it begins to wilt, until the broccoli rabe is tender but still bright green, about 5 minutes. Uncover and cook until the water evaporates, 3–5 minutes. Drizzle with olive oil and season to taste with salt.

Serve the sausage and broccoli rabe together.

GRILLED VEAL BIRDS
serves 4–6

When rolled up and skewered, these *involtini* are thought to resemble little headless birds—leave it to the Italians to think up such a fanciful name!

¼ cup extra-virgin olive oil, plus more for drizzling

1 large onion, finely chopped

3 tablespoons dried currants

½ cup fresh bread crumbs

Salt and pepper

¼ teaspoon crushed red pepper flakes

¼ cup finely grated pecorino

12 veal cutlets, about 1½ pounds

Lemon wedges

Soak 8–12 wooden skewers in a pan of water to keep them from singeing on the grill.

Heat the olive oil in a medium skillet over medium heat. Add the onions and cook, stirring often, until softened, 10–15 minutes. Stir in the currants, then push the onions and currants to the sides of the skillet. Add the bread crumbs to the center and cook, stirring frequently, until golden, 5–10 minutes. Stir the onions and currants into the bread crumbs. Season with salt and pepper, and add the red pepper flakes. Set aside to cool, then stir in the pecorino. This makes 1½ cups of filling.

Use the smooth side of a meat pounder on a sturdy work surface and pound each veal cutlet into roughly a 4 × 6-inch rectangle. Season with salt and pepper. Spread about 2 tablespoons of the bread crumb filling evenly over the meat. Working with one cutlet at a time and starting with a narrow side, fold in the sides to keep the filling contained and roll up the cutlet like a jelly roll. Repeat with the remaining cutlets and filling until there are 12 involtini.

Thread up to 4 involtini onto 2 parallel wooden skewers set about 1 inch apart, leaving an inch or two between each veal piece. (Doubling up on the skewers prevents the involtini from swiveling on the skewers.) Drizzle the skewered involtini with olive oil and season with salt and pepper.

Prepare a medium-hot charcoal or gas grill. Grill the involtini until browned on both sides, 1–1½ minutes per side. Transfer to a serving platter. Season with salt and pepper and drizzle with olive oil. Serve with lemon wedges.

BRAISED PORK WITH ROMANO & STRING BEANS
serves 6

The beauty of this dish is that from so little effort, comes such tender, flavorful meat with lots of fragrant juices. Pork shoulder is a tough cut (it comes from a "working" or well-exercised part of the pig), so we cook it long and slow until it is fork-tender.

FOR THE PORK
1 boneless pork shoulder or butt, 3–4 pounds
Salt and pepper
Zest of 1 lemon, peeled in wide strips
2 tablespoons extra-virgin olive oil, plus more for drizzling

FOR THE BEANS
1 pound Romano beans, trimmed and strings removed
½ pound green string beans, trimmed
½ pound yellow string beans, trimmed

For the pork, lay the meat out on a work surface, fat side down. Season it with plenty of salt and pepper. Tuck the lemon zest into the creases and folds. Gather the loose folds of the pork together to enclose the seasonings and make a neat package by trussing the roast shut with kitchen string. Rub salt and pepper all over the meat. Slide the pork in a resealable plastic bag and seal, squeezing out all of the air. Refrigerate overnight or up to 2 days.

Preheat the oven to 200°. Slip the pork out of the bag and put it in a large enameled cast-iron or other heavy pot with a tight-fitting lid. Rub olive oil all over the meat. Cover the pot. Roast the pork (resisting the urge to peek at it as it cooks) until fragrant, very tender, and lots of juices have accumulated in the pot, about 8 hours.

For the beans, bring a large pot of salted water to a bowl over high heat. Add the Romano beans and cook for 5 minutes. Add the string beans and cook until the Romano and the string beans are very tender, about 15 minutes. Drain.

Remove the pork from the oven and transfer to a cutting board. Add the beans to the juices in the pot, then cover to keep warm. Carve the meat (the slices will fall apart somewhat) and arrange on a serving platter along with the beans. Spoon the fragrant pot juices over the beans and pork. Drizzle with olive oil.

PORK CHOPS & MARINATED ROASTED PEPPERS
serves 4

It's funny how our mood will swing between wanting thin pork chops or thicker, juicier ones, without rhyme or reason. We like the thin chops precisely because they're thin and have the chewy texture of a cutlet. (They're also less expensive.) They need to cook quickly in a hot skillet—in and out—to keep from getting tough. Thicker, meatier chops can be nice and juicy if the pork quality is good and they're not overcooked. Choose the thickness that suits you, but keep in mind that the marinated roasted peppers are good and meaty, so you may want to lean toward using thin-cut chops.

4 pork chops
Extra-virgin olive oil
Salt and pepper

1 recipe Marinated Roasted Peppers (see page 30)

Rub the pork chops with a little olive oil and season both sides with salt and pepper. Put a splash of olive oil into a heavy large skillet over medium-high heat. Put the chops in the skillet in a single layer and pan-fry until well browned, 3–5 minutes per side. If using thin-cut chops, transfer them to a platter. If cooking thick-cut pork chops, reduce the heat to medium and continue cooking the chops until the juices run clear when pierced near the bone, 3–5 minutes, then transfer to a platter.

Season the chops with a little salt and pepper. Spoon the marinated peppers and their juices over the pork chops. Serve warm or at room temperature.

eat
your
verdure

AVOCADOS WITH LEMON-SUPREME VINAIGRETTE

Slice the ends off of 1 lemon. Stand the lemon up on one end and cut off the rind and white pith, exposing the flesh. Working over a salad bowl, cut along both sides of each segment to release it from its membrane, letting it drop into the bowl. Add 2 minced anchovy filets, 1 pinch crushed red pepper flakes, and ¼ cup really good extra-virgin olive oil to the bowl. Season with salt and pepper. Stir well, mashing up the lemon segments with the back of a spoon to break them up. Slice 2 ripe Hass avocados in half lengthwise. Remove the pit and peel each avocado half. Spoon the vinaigrette into 4 avocado halves. — *serves 2–4*

CAULIFLOWER SALAD WITH GREEN OLIVES, RADISHES & PARSLEY
serves 4–6

We serve this pretty vegetable salad—with its bright lemony vinaigrette, meaty olives, and crunchy, peppery radishes—on its own or with smoky grilled birds, meats, or fish.

1 clove garlic, minced
Juice of 2 lemons (about ¼ cup)
Salt and pepper
5–6 tablespoons really good
   extra-virgin olive oil,
   plus more for drizzling
1 head cauliflower, cored and
   broken into small florets

1 small bunch radishes, quartered
   or sliced
½ cup green olives, pitted and torn
   in half
1 handful fresh parsley leaves,
   chopped
Pinch of crushed red pepper flakes

Put the garlic, lemon juice, and salt and pepper to taste in a large bowl. Whisk in the olive oil. Taste the vinaigrette, adjust the seasonings, and set aside.

Cook the cauliflower in a large pot of salted boiling water over medium-high heat until tender, about 4 minutes. Drain well, then add to the bowl with the vinaigrette. Gently toss, then let marinate at room temperature for 1 hour.

Add the radishes, olives, parsley, and red pepper flakes to the cauliflower. Season to taste with salt and pepper. Drizzle each serving with a little olive oil.

ROMANO BEANS IN TOMATO SAUCE

We've both had terrific luck growing flat, green Romano beans in our home gardens. Every spring we plant the "magic" seeds and by midsummer the stalks are so tall and vigorous, it seems they could keep growing clear up to the sky; a stepladder is the only way to reach the beans at the top. These are stewing beans—they need to simmer for a time to become tender, and we like ours soft.

Put 1 pound Romano beans, 2–3 cloves crushed, peeled garlic, 4 cups passata di pomodoro or strained tomatoes, ¼–½ cup extra-virgin olive oil, 2 sprigs fresh basil, ½ cup water, and salt and pepper to taste into a heavy, medium, nonreactive pot with a tight-fitting lid. Bring to a simmer over medium heat. Reduce the heat to maintain a gentle simmer. Stew the beans in the sauce, stirring occasionally, until they are very tender, 45–60 minutes. Adjust the seasonings. Serve the beans with lots of the flavorful sauce. —— *serves 6*

STRING BEAN SALAD WITH HAZELNUTS & CREAM
serves 4

Most nuts benefit from toasting to bring out their rich, nutty flavor. Toast the hazelnuts for this salad in a 400° oven until golden brown.

1 pound string beans	Salt and pepper
⅓ cup heavy cream	Juice of 1 lemon
2 teaspoons finely grated lemon zest	½ cup toasted, skinless hazelnuts, coarsely chopped

Cook the string beans in a large pot of salted boiling water over medium-high heat until tender, about 8 minutes. Drain the beans, then rinse them under cool water. Put the beans in the refrigerator until they are cold.

Combine the cream and lemon zest in a large bowl. Season with salt and pepper. Whisk in the lemon juice. The sauce will thicken, but it won't curdle.

Add the beans and hazelnuts to the bowl and toss well. Add a splash of water to loosen the sauce if it's too thick. Adjust the seasonings. Serve cold.

PEPPERS ROASTED WITH ANCHOVIES & BUTTER
serves 2–4

Each bite of these pretty cupped peppers is a mouthful of flavor. Gild the lily and add the cream.

2 medium red bell peppers, cored, quartered lengthwise, and seeded
4 anchovy filets
2 cloves garlic, thinly sliced
2 tablespoons butter, cut into pieces

Really good extra-virgin olive oil
Salt and pepper
2 teaspoons heavy cream, optional
1 tablespoon finely chopped fresh parsley leaves

Preheat the oven to 325°. Arrange the peppers flesh side up in a single layer in a shallow baking dish. Tear each anchovy filet in half and tuck one piece, along with 2 or 3 slices of garlic, in each pepper. Divide the pieces of butter evenly between the peppers. Drizzle the peppers with olive oil, and season to taste with salt and pepper. Go easy on the salt; the anchovies are good and salty.

Roast the peppers until the flesh has softened but is not completely tender, 30–40 minutes. Remove the peppers from the oven. Drizzle with heavy cream, if you like. Scatter the peppers with parsley. Serve warm.

ZUCCHINI WITH SPICY ANCHOVY BUTTER

We first started serving this sauce years ago spooned over fat shrimp that had been grilled in their shells over hardwood coals. We'd peel and eat the shrimp, dipping them in the sauce, licking the deliciousness off our fingers. It was so addictive we found ourselves putting more sauce onto the plate so we could mop it up with hunks of warm bread. Why stop at shrimp? Now we spoon it on steamed spinach, roasted beets, or cooked vegetables like these.

Cook ½ pound baby zucchini in a medium pot of salted boiling water over medium-high heat until very tender but not falling apart, about 8 minutes. Drain. Return the empty pot to the stove. Reduce the heat to medium-low. Melt 6 tablespoons butter in the pot. Add 6 minced anchovy filets and 2 pinches of crushed red pepper flakes, swirling the pot. Add the zucchini, turning them to coat. Season with a little salt, if you like. Serve warm. —— *serves 4*

Overleaf, top row, left to right: Romano Beans in Tomato Sauce, Green Pea & Prosciutto Frittata, Peppers Roasted with Anchovies & Butter, Avocados with Lemon-Supreme Vinaigrette; bottom row, left to right: Zucchini with Spicy Anchovy Butter, Tomatoes with Tonnato Sauce, Potatoes with Anchovies & Red Pepper Flakes, lunch in Palermo

TOMATOES WITH TONNATO SAUCE
serves 4–6

We love this sauce so much we spoon it on everything—boiled potatoes, grilled chicken, steamed summer vegetables hot or cold—but our favorite is this beautiful ode to tomato season.

FOR THE TONNATO SAUCE
2 large egg yolks
Salt
Juice of ½ lemon
½ cup canola oil
½ cup really good extra-virgin olive oil
1 small can tuna packed in olive oil (about 2 ounces), preferably Italian
3 anchovy filets

1 tablespoon capers
1 clove garlic
Pepper

FOR THE TOMATOES
2 pounds tomatoes of various types and sizes, cored and sliced or halved
Arugula leaves
Salt and pepper
Really good extra-virgin olive oil

For the tonnato sauce, whisk together the egg yolks, a pinch of salt, and half of the lemon juice in a medium bowl. Combine the canola and olive oils in a measuring cup with a spout. Whisking constantly, add the oil to the yolks, about 1 teaspoon at a time. The sauce will thicken and emulsify. After you've added about ¼ cup of the oil, you can begin to slowly drizzle in the remaining oil as you continue to whisk, until you have a thick glossy mayonnaise. Transfer the sauce to a small bowl.

Purée the tuna, anchovies, capers, and garlic in a food processor until it is a smooth paste. Add a little olive oil to help the process. Use a rubber spatula and press the tuna paste through a sieve into the mayonnaise. Season to taste with the remaining lemon juice and salt and pepper. Transfer to a covered container and refrigerate until ready to use. The sauce will keep for up to 1 week in the refrigerator.

For the tomatoes, spoon some of the sauce onto individual plates or a platter and arrange the tomatoes on top. Spoon more sauce over the tomatoes. Scatter the arugula on top. Season with salt and pepper and a drizzle of olive oil.

TOMATOES STUFFED WITH TUNA SALAD
makes 4

This tuna salad will keep in the refrigerator for a couple of days, but the flavors are best at room temperature, when the salad has just been made. Tomatoes should always stay out of the fridge. The cold saps their flavor and texture.

4 ripe tomatoes

Salt

Two 5-ounce cans tuna packed in olive oil, drained

1 large handful fresh parsley leaves, chopped

4 scallions, thinly sliced

3 tablespoons really good extra-virgin olive oil, plus more for drizzling

Juice of ½–1 lemon

Pepper

1 hard-boiled egg, peeled and coarsely chopped

Slice off the top quarter of each tomato. Use a small spoon to carefully scoop out and discard the interior pulp without piercing the tomato walls. Sprinkle the inside of each tomato with a pinch of salt, then turn the tomatoes upside down on a paper towel to drain.

Put the tuna in a medium bowl, flaking it with your fingers or a fork. Fold in the parsley, scallions, olive oil, and lemon juice. Season with salt and pepper. Add the hard-boiled egg, mixing gently. Fill each tomato with some of the tuna salad. Drizzle the tomatoes with olive oil before serving.

POTATOES WITH ANCHOVIES & RED PEPPER FLAKES

Put 2–3 russet potatoes in a medium pot, cover with cold water, and add a generous pinch of salt. Bring to a boil over high heat, then reduce the heat to medium. Simmer the potatoes until tender when pierced, 30–40 minutes. Drain. When cool enough to handle, peel the potatoes. Meanwhile, heat ¼ cup extra-virgin olive oil, 6 minced anchovy filets, and 1 teaspoon crushed red pepper flakes in a small saucepan over medium heat, stirring often, until the oil is very warm and the anchovies have dissolved, 3–5 minutes.

Slice the warm potatoes into thick rounds and arrange them on a serving platter. Spoon the warm oil over the potatoes. —*serves 4*

EGGPLANT COOKED IN THE COALS

Prepare a hardwood charcoal fire. When the coals are medium hot, put 4 small or 2 medium whole eggplant directly on the coals. Cook the eggplant, turning them as the skin blackens and turns papery, until they begin to collapse and the flesh is soft, 5–15 minutes depending on the size of eggplant and the heat of the coals. Transfer the eggplant to a wire rack on a sheet pan. When they are cool enough to handle, peel off the blackened skin, leaving the flesh whole and the stem end intact. Return the eggplant to the wire rack and let them drain for about 30 minutes before serving. —— *serves 4–6*

EGGPLANT WITH SMOKY TOMATO & HARISSA SAUCE
serves 4–6

There are many sensuous flavors in this sauce. We sometimes spoon it over chicken or fish (or abandon ourselves and just eat it by the spoonful).

For the sauce
2 small ripe tomatoes
3 anchovy filets, minced
1 clove garlic, peeled and minced
1 teaspoon harissa
1 teaspoon red wine vinegar
2 tablespoons extra-virgin olive oil

For the eggplant
4 small or 2 medium eggplant, charred, peeled, and drained (see above)
Extra-virgin olive oil
Salt
1 small handful fresh parsley leaves, chopped
1 lemon, quartered

For the sauce, grill the tomatoes over a hot charcoal fire until the skin blackens and splits, and before the tomatoes collapse, 2–3 minutes. Put the tomatoes in a sieve over a bowl. Press the juice and flesh through; discard the skin. Put ¼ cup of the pulpy tomato juices in a medium bowl. Add the anchovies, garlic, harissa, and vinegar. Stir in the olive oil. Adjust the seasonings.

For the eggplant, spoon half the sauce onto a serving platter. Place the eggplant on top. Spoon the remaining sauce over the eggplant. Let the flavors meld for a bit. Drizzle with olive oil. Season with salt. Garnish with parsley and lemons and serve with hunks of warm country bread or grilled flatbread, if you like.

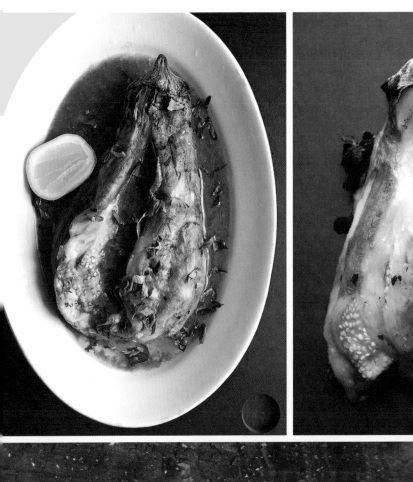

GREEN PEA & PROSCIUTTO FRITTATA
serves 6

We usually have a dozen eggs and a hunk of parmigiano stashed in our fridge. And sometimes, the only green vegetable we've got on hand is a bag of frozen peas. This frittata is a staple at Canal House when we're hungry and need to scrape together something good to eat with very little.

4 tablespoons extra-virgin olive oil

1 small onion, finely chopped

4 ounces (6 thin slices) prosciutto, coarsely chopped

Salt and pepper

2 cups peas, blanched if fresh; defrosted if frozen

1 large handful fresh parsley leaves, finely chopped

1 cup finely grated parmigiano-reggiano

6 eggs

Heat 2 tablespoons of the oil in a large, well-seasoned cast-iron or nonstick skillet over medium heat. Add the onions and cook until they begin to soften, about 5 minutes. Add the prosciutto and cook until the onions are soft, 5–8 minutes. Season with salt and pepper (prosciutto is salty so be sparing with the salt and lavish with the pepper, if you like). Using a rubber spatula, scrape the onions and prosciutto into a large bowl. Wipe the skillet clean with a paper towel and set the skillet aside.

Add the peas, parsley, and parmigiano to the bowl with the onions and stir well. Crack the eggs into a medium bowl, add a pinch of salt, and beat the eggs well. Pour the eggs into the bowl with the peas, stirring until well combined.

Heat 1 tablespoon of the oil in the reserved skillet over medium heat. When the skillet is hot, pour in the egg mixture, smoothing the top with a spatula. Cook until the bottom of the frittata is golden and set, 10–12 minutes. Slide the frittata out of the skillet onto a large plate. Add the remaining 1 tablespoon oil to the skillet, swirling it to coat.

Carefully invert the frittata into the skillet, browned side facing up. Return the skillet to medium heat. Continue cooking the frittata until the bottom is golden, about 5 minutes. Slide the frittata onto a serving platter. Season with a little salt. Slice into wedges. Serve warm or room temperature.

ZUCCHINI PANCAKES
makes about 12

When zucchini season hits, farm market bins bulge and the zucchini plants in our gardens start producing like they're growing in Jurassic Park. That's when we make these pancakes. They go as fast as the zucchini come on.

4 medium zucchini
Salt
8 eggs
1 cup finely grated pecorino
½ cup all-purpose flour
1 bunch scallions, thinly sliced
1 large handful fresh parsley leaves, finely chopped

1 clove garlic, minced
Finely grated zest of 2 lemons
Big pinch of crushed red pepper flakes
Pepper
Olive oil

Working over a colander set over a large bowl, grate the zucchini on the large holes of a box grater into the colander. Generously sprinkle salt over the grated zucchini and toss with your hands. Set the zucchini aside to drain for 30 minutes. Discard the liquid. Squeeze the zucchini by the handful to get as much liquid out as possible.

Crack the eggs into a large mixing bowl and lightly beat them. Add the zucchini, pecorino, flour, scallions, parsley, garlic, lemon zest, and red pepper flakes. Season with salt and pepper. Gently stir until well combined.

Heat 1 tablespoon of olive oil in a heavy large skillet over medium heat until hot but not smoking. For each pancake, spoon about ¼ cup of batter into the skillet at least 2 inches apart. Cook until little holes appear on the surface and the cooked side of the pancakes—lift the edges to check—are golden brown, 1–2 minutes. Turn the pancakes over and cook until the second side is golden brown, 1–2 minutes. Transfer as done to a wire rack. Repeat with the remaining batter, making about 12 pancakes. Add more oil to the skillet as needed. Serve warm.

WHITE BEANS WITH SPICY BLACK OLIVE VINAIGRETTE
serves 2–4

When we use canned beans, we like to give them a little love before we dress them. Drain them into a sieve, give them a good rinse under cold running water, then drain well and toss with a drizzle of olive oil and season with salt. Then go in with your dressing.

½ clove garlic, minced
¼ cup finely chopped pitted black olives
1 tablespoon finely chopped parsley leaves
1 tablespoon red wine vinegar

¼ cup really good extra-virgin olive oil, plus more for drizzling
Pinch of crushed red pepper flakes
Salt and pepper
2 cups cooked cannellini beans

Stir together the garlic, olives, parsley, vinegar, olive oil, and red pepper flakes in a medium mixing bowl. Season with salt and pepper. Add the beans and toss gently to coat. Taste and adjust the seasonings. Transfer to a serving platter and drizzle with more olive oil before serving.

COOKING DRIED BEANS

Look for the "Best if Used By" date when buying a package of dried beans. The fresher the beans, the more quickly they'll cook. Cook a whole pound, it will yield 4–5 cups of beans. Add them to salads or just serve them as a side dish dressed with a little olive oil and fresh lemon juice. Cooked beans freeze beautifully.

TO COOK BEANS: Put the dried beans in a large pot and add enough cold water to cover by 4 inches. Cover and bring to a rolling boil over high heat. Turn off the heat and allow the beans to soak undisturbed for about 1 hour. Drain the beans and add fresh water to cover by 2 inches. Bring to a gentle boil over high heat, then reduce the heat to medium-low and cook until the beans are tender. It can take anywhere from 1–3 hours, depending on the freshness of the beans. Test them after an hour to see how they are progressing. Add salt and let them cool in their liquid.

Pizza ◦ Pizza ◦ Pizza

PIZZA DOUGH
makes four 10-inch pizzas

This pizza dough can be made early in the day and left to slowly rise in the refrigerator until the evening; you can even leave it overnight. Use this dough with any of the following recipes or with your own pizza toppings.

1 envelope active dry yeast (2¼ teaspoons)

3 tablespoons really good extra-virgin olive oil, plus more for the crust

4 cups bread flour, plus more for kneading

2 teaspoons salt, plus more for the crust

Cornmeal

For the dough, dissolve the yeast in ½ cup warm water in a small bowl. Stir in 1¼ cups water and 2 tablespoons of the olive oil.

Pulse the flour and salt together in a food processor. Pour the yeast mixture through the feed hole in the lid while the processor is running and process until the dough comes together and forms a sticky ball, about 1 minute. Turn the dough out on a floured work surface and briefly knead into a smooth ball. Put the remaining 1 tablespoon oil in a large bowl. Roll the dough around in the bowl until coated all over with oil. Cover the bowl with plastic wrap and let the dough rise in a warm spot until it has doubled in size, about 2 hours.

Divide the dough into 4 equal pieces on a lightly floured surface and shape each into a ball. Place the balls at least 5 inches apart, loosely cover them with a clean, damp kitchen towel, and let them rise until nearly doubled in size, 30–60 minutes.

Place a pizza stone on the upper rack in the oven and preheat the oven to 500°. Working with one ball at a time, stretch the dough into a 10-inch round on a floured surface, letting it rest and relax if resistant. Lay the dough out on a cornmeal-dusted pizza peel or a rimless cookie sheet. Prick the surface with a fork, drizzle with some olive oil, and sprinkle with salt. Arrange the pizza toppings of your choosing on the dough. Slide the pizza off the peel onto the hot pizza stone in the oven. Bake until the crust is puffed and golden around the edges and the topping is bubbling hot, 6–8 minutes. Use the peel to remove the pizza from the oven.

GRILLED PIZZA MARGHERITA

It's too hot in the summer to be trapped indoors making pizza with the oven blasting away at 500°. Take it outside! Fire up a charcoal grill and make these smoky grilled flatbreads (an ancient method, after all). This is our favorite grilled pizza, but try your hand at other toppings too.

Follow the instructions for Pizza Dough (see page 104) through the second step.

Prepare a medium-hot hardwood charcoal or gas grill. Meanwhile, turn the pizza dough out onto a well-floured work surface. Tear or cut the dough into six pieces and shape each into a ball. Cover with a clean, damp kitchen towel and let the dough relax for 5–30 minutes. Stretch the first ball of dough into a ½-inch-thick free-form disk, letting it rest and relax if resistant. Let the dough relax briefly, then stretch it out further until it is about ¼ inch thick and 8–10 inches in diameter. Slide the dough onto a floured pizza peel or rimless cookie sheet and prick all over with a fork.

Slide the dough onto the grill (don't worry, the dough will not ooze through the grate!) over the medium-hot coals. Grill until the crust is set and the bottom has dark brown grill marks, about 1 minute. Using long tongs, transfer the crust to a clean surface, brush with some oil, and turn grilled side up. Repeat rolling and grilling process with the remaining balls of dough.

To assemble and finish grilling the pizza, spoon a thin film (about ¼ cup) of Raw Tomato Sauce (see page 109) over the crust, cover with 4–6 slices of fresh mozzarella, drizzle with really good extra-virgin olive oil, and scatter some basil leaves on top. Slide the pizza back onto the grill. Cover with the grill lid and grill the pizza until the cheese melts and the bottom of the pizza is crisp and browned, about 2 minutes.

Serve the pizzas hot off the grill, allowing them to rest briefly before slicing them into wedges. —— *makes 6 pizzas*

Preceding pages, left: making pizza at Canal House; right: a woman carrying a pizza to the local communal oven in Castel Vittorio, a mountainside village in Liguria

PROSCIUTTO, LEMON & OLIVE PIZZA

Arrange 3 ounces torn fresh mozzarella and 8 paper-thin lemon slices over the prepared pizza dough. Scatter 6–8 halved, pitted green olives and the leaves of 1 sprig fresh rosemary on top and sprinkle with a pinch of Aleppo pepper. Bake the pizza until the cheese is melted and bubbling, 6–8 minutes. Remove the pizza from the oven. Drape 3 thin slices prosciutto over the hot pizza, drizzle with a little really good extra-virgin olive oil, and cut into wedges. —— *makes 1 pizza*

WHITE CLAM PIZZA

Heat 2 tablespoons extra-virgin olive oil, 2 thinly sliced cloves of garlic, and a pinch of crushed red pepper flakes in a small skillet over medium heat until everything begins to sizzle, about 2 minutes. Stir in ¼ cup drained, canned baby clams and a splash of the juice from the can, and season with salt to taste. Set aside. Using a vegetable peeler, make long shards of cheese from a 1-ounce hunk of parmigiano-reggiano. Scatter the cheese over the prepared pizza dough, then spoon the seasoned clams evenly over the top. Brush the edges of the dough with more olive oil. Bake the pizza until the cheese is melted and the clams are bubbling, 6–8 minutes. Remove the pizza from the oven. Drizzle with a little more olive oil, and cut into wedges. —— *makes 1 pizza*

POTATO & ONION PIZZA

Use a mandoline to thinly slice 2 Yukon gold potatoes. Wash the potato slices in several changes of cold water until the water runs clear. Drain the potatoes, toss with a generous pinch of salt, and transfer to a colander to drain and soften for about 10 minutes. Transfer the potatoes to a medium bowl. Add 1 small onion, sliced lengthwise. Add 2 tablespoons really good extra-virgin olive oil, season to taste with salt, and toss with your hands until the potatoes and onions are well coated. Set aside for about 5 minutes. Arrange the potatoes in overlapping circles over the prepared pizza dough, tucking slices of onion in between. Sprinkle a big pinch of crushed red pepper flakes over the pizza, then brush the edges of the dough with more olive oil. Bake until the potatoes are tender and the crust is golden, 6–8 minutes. Remove the pizza from the oven. Drizzle with a little more olive oil, and cut into wedges. —— *makes 1 pizza*

ESCAROLE, FONTINA & BLACK OLIVE PIZZA

Rinse ¼ head of escarole. Coarsely chop the wet leaves (you should have about 4 cups). Heat 1 tablespoon extra-virgin olive oil in a medium skillet over medium heat. Add the wet leaves, season to taste with salt, and cook, stirring often, until they are limp, 2–3 minutes. Drain the escarole, then scatter the leaves, about ¼ cup grated Italian fontina, and a small handful of pitted, black oil-cured olives over the prepared pizza dough. Bake the pizza until the cheese is melted, 6–8 minutes. Remove the pizza from the oven. Drizzle with a little really good extra-virgin olive oil, and cut into wedges. —— *makes 1 pizza*

PIZZA WITH HARISSA MUSSELS

Drizzle some really good extra-virgin olive oil over the prepared pizza dough and sprinkle with ½ cup finely grated parmigiano-reggiano. Bake the pizza until the cheese is melted and the crust is golden brown, about 6 minutes. Remove the pizza from the oven. Spoon a half recipe of Harissa Mussels (see page 63) and their flavorful juices over the pizza. Cut into wedges. —— *makes 1 pizza*

RAW TOMATO SAUCE

This recipe makes 4 cups of sauce and since you only need about ¼ cup for each little pizza, there will be leftover sauce. Don't worry, it is money in the bank. The sauce keeps nicely in the refrigerator for up to 1 week, freezes beautifully, or use it to make Hot Spaghetti Tossed with Raw Tomato Sauce (see page 38).

Halve lengthwise 1½–2 pounds ripe plum tomatoes. Grate the cut sides of the tomatoes on the large holes of a box grater into a large bowl, discarding the skin. Add 1–2 finely chopped cloves garlic, ½ cup passata di pomodoro, strained tomatoes, or tomato purée, and 4–6 tablespoons really good extra-virgin olive oil. Season with salt and pepper. —— *makes about 4 cups*

Dolci

WINE-POACHED APRICOTS WITH RICOTTA
serves 6

We planted bronze fennel (*Foeniculum vulgare* 'Purpureum'), which is a culinary herb, in our garden a few years ago and it took off. Each spring it comes back fuller and more vigorous than the year before. By midsummer, the tall feathery plants are blooming lacy yellow flowers (which eventually bear the tiny aromatic seeds we cook with), just as the apricots appear at our local orchard. We love the combination of these two flavors: the perfumed apricots and licorice of the fennel. We keep some of the flavorful syrup from the apricots to make a refreshing drink with bubbly prosecco, or with sparkling water over ice.

FOR THE APRICOTS
1 bottle white wine
1½ cups sugar
4 branches fennel fronds, preferably
  with their flowering heads
6 black peppercorns
1½ pounds apricots, halved and
  pitted

FOR THE RICOTTA
2 cups finest fresh ricotta
1 tablespoon sugar

For the apricots, put the wine and sugar into a heavy, wide pot. Bring to a simmer over medium heat, stirring often, until the sugar dissolves. Add the fennel fronds, peppercorns, and apricots to the hot syrup. Simmer until the fruit has softened but still holds its shape, 2–3 minutes. Remove the pot from the heat. Let the apricots cool in the syrup, stirring gently from time to time. Discard the fennel fronds and peppercorns. The apricots will keep in their syrup in the refrigerator for up to 5 days.

For the ricotta, using a wooden spoon, mix together the ricotta and sugar in a medium bowl until well blended. Keep refrigerated until ready to serve.

To serve, divide the ricotta between 6 dessert dishes and spoon some of the apricots and their syrup over them.

RASPBERRY TART WITH MASCARPONE CREAM
makes one 11-inch tart

This elegant tart with its buttery, almond-flecked crust is good any time of year, but made with juicy raspberries in season, it's *really* good!

FOR THE CRUST
1½ cups all-purpose flour
½ cup almond meal or almond flour
¼ cup sugar
1 teaspoon salt
8 tablespoons cold unsalted butter
1 whole egg
1 egg yolk
1 tablespoon white wine

FOR THE FILLING AND CREAM
½ cup seedless raspberry jam
2 pints (4–5 cups) fresh raspberries
3 tablespoons superfine sugar
1½ cups mascarpone
Finely grated zest of 1 small orange
1 tablespoon kirsch

For the crust, whisk the flour, almond meal, sugar, and salt together in a large mixing bowl. Cut the butter into the flour mixture using a pastry blender or 2 butter knives until it resembles wet sand. Lightly beat the egg and egg yolk together with the wine in a small bowl. Stir the egg mixture into the flour mixture with a fork. Press the dough together until it forms a rough ball. Try not to overhandle the dough or the crust will be tough. Shape the dough into a flat disk, wrap in plastic wrap, and refrigerate for at least 1 hour.

Roll out the dough on a lightly floured surface into a thin 13-inch round. Roll the dough around the rolling pin, then unfurl it into an 11-inch fluted tart pan with removable bottom. Trim off any excess dough and crimp the edges. Prick the dough with a fork, then refrigerate for 30 minutes.

Preheat the oven to 375°. Line the crust with parchment paper or foil and fill with pie weights. Bake until pale brown, 20 minutes. Remove the parchment paper and pie weights from the crust and bake until the crust is golden brown, about 20 minutes. Transfer to a wire rack to cool slightly.

For the filling and cream, spread the jam over the bottom of the warm crust. Arrange the berries in a single layer on top of the jam. Sprinkle the tart with 1 tablespoon of the sugar. Combine the mascarpone, orange zest, remaining 2 tablespoons sugar, and kirsch in a mixing bowl. Serve the tart with the cream.

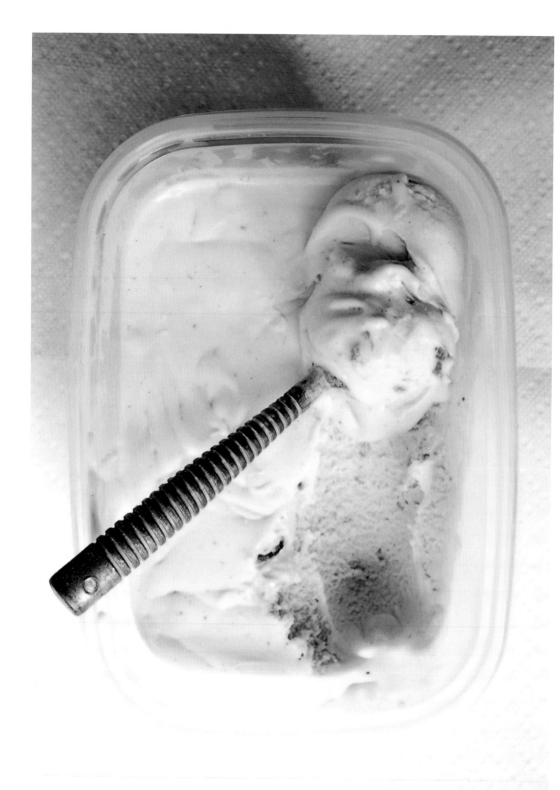

FIG GELATO
makes 1 quart

We have several fledgling fig trees that bear beautiful leaves and, if we're lucky, a handful of fruit. Fig country we do not live in! But we love their jammy sweetness so we make this exquisite gelato with preserves. As we eat it, we close our eyes and pretend that the rich fig flavor came from our very own figs from our very own trees.

2 cups whole milk
1 cup heavy cream
¾ cup sugar
6 egg yolks

Pinch of salt
1 cup fig preserves
2 teaspoons vanilla bean paste or vanilla extract

Put the milk, cream, and ½ cup of the sugar into a heavy saucepan and bring to a simmer over medium heat, stirring gently until the sugar dissolves.

Meanwhile, put the egg yolks, salt, and the remaining ¼ cup of sugar into a medium mixing bowl and whisk together until the yolks are thick and pale yellow.

Gradually ladle about 1 cup of the hot milk into the yolks, whisking constantly. Stir the warm yolk mixture into the hot milk in the saucepan. Reduce the heat to low and cook, stirring constantly, until the custard is thick enough to coat the back of the spoon and registers between 175° and 180° on an instant-read thermometer, about 10 minutes. Stirring the custard constantly as it cooks and thickens prevents it from coming to a boil and curdling.

Strain the custard into a medium bowl. Stir in the fig preserves and vanilla. Set the bowl into a larger bowl filled with ice, then stir the custard frequently until it has cooled. Cover the custard and refrigerate it until completely chilled, about 4 hours (it can keep in the refrigerator for up to 2 days).

Churn the custard in an ice-cream maker following the manufacturer's instructions. Scoop the gelato (it will have the consistency of soft-serve) into a quart container with a lid, cover, and freeze for a couple of hours until it is just firm. If you serve the gelato after it is frozen solid, let it soften before serving. It will keep for up to 2 days in the freezer.

ALMOND MILK ICE CREAM
makes about 1 quart

We like our ice cream rich, yet this one, despite lacking eggs or heavy cream, is a favorite. It's smooth and full of flavor, but lighter and more refreshing than a custard-based ice cream. When we are pressed for time, or are feeling lazy (God forbid!), we make the quick version of this recipe provided below.

1½ cups whole almonds   1 cup sugar
4 cups whole milk   2 tablespoons honey

Put the almonds in a food processor and pulse until they are finely ground, being careful not to grind them to a paste. Set aside.

Put the milk and sugar into a heavy medium saucepan. Heat over medium heat, stirring frequently, until the sugar dissolves and the milk is hot. Take care not to let the milk come to a boil. Remove the pan from the heat and stir the ground almonds into the hot milk. Set it aside to cool. Transfer to a bowl, cover with plastic wrap, and refrigerate overnight.

Line a medium sieve with a large double-thick layer of cheesecloth and set the sieve over a deep bowl. Pour the almonds and milk through the cheesecloth. Gather up the ends and wring out as much of the milk as possible into the bowl. Discard the nuts. Stir the honey into the milk.

Churn the almond milk in an ice-cream maker following the manufacturer's directions. Scoop the ice cream into a quart container with a lid, cover, and freeze until just firm. The ice cream will keep for up to 3 days in the freezer.

QUICK ALMOND MILK ICE CREAM

Combine 4 cups unsweetened almond milk, 1 cup superfine sugar, 2 tablespoons honey, and ¼ teaspoon almond extract in a large mixing bowl, stirring until the sugar dissolves. Cover with plastic wrap and refrigerate until well chilled, about 4 hours. Churn the almond milk in an ice-cream maker following the manufacturer's directions. Scoop the ice cream into a quart container with a lid, cover, and freeze until just firm. The ice cream will keep for up to 3 days in the freezer. —— *makes about 1 quart*

ALMOND COOKIES
makes about 20

The recipe for these cookies is based on the classic Sienese *ricciarelli*, a staple of the dessert table at Christmas. In the summer, we serve them with ripe cherries, peaches, and apricots. And year-round we dip these delicate cookies into our cups of our afternoon espresso.

2 cups whole blanched almonds	1 teaspoon vanilla extract
¾ cup sugar	½ teaspoon almond extract
Finely grated zest of 1 orange	2 egg whites
Finely grated zest of 1 lemon	Pinch of cream of tartar

Preheat the oven to 325°. Put the almonds and ½ cup of the sugar in a food processor and pulse until the almonds are finely ground, being careful not to grind them to a paste. Add the citrus zests and the extracts and pulse a few times to combine. Transfer the ground almonds to a large mixing bowl.

Whisk the egg whites and cream of tartar together in a medium mixing bowl until they hold soft peaks. Gradually add the remaining ¼ cup sugar, whisking constantly, until the whites hold stiff but not dry peaks. Gently fold the egg whites into the ground almonds. The dough will be soft and moist. Using two smallish soup spoons, shape the dough into small quenelles or ovoids, arranging them at least 1 inch apart on cookie sheets lined with parchment paper.

Bake the cookies until puffed and pale golden brown, about 20 minutes. Remove the cookies from the oven and when cool enough to handle, peel them off the paper and transfer them to a wire rack to cool completely.

VARIATION: To make one large "cookie" tart, spread the almond cookie dough into an ungreased 9-inch fluted tart pan with a removable bottom and smooth out the top. Press about ⅓ cup blanched almonds decoratively around the edge of the dough, if you like. Scatter ½ cup sliced almonds over the center of the dough, gently pressing them in. Bake until puffed and pale golden brown, about 30 minutes. Loosen the cookie from the sides of the tart pan while still warm, then transfer it to a wire rack to cool. To serve, cut into wedges or break into roughly shaped pieces and serve dusted with powdered sugar, if you like.

BISCOTTI DI ANICE
makes about 4 dozen cookies

We grew up adoring those Stella D'oro aniseed biscuits, long before biscotti (a word most Americans had never even heard of back then) became the rage. These fine biscotti remind us of those biscuits, and taste even better.

2 cups plus 1 tablespoon
  all-purpose flour
½ teaspoon baking powder
½ teaspoon baking soda
3 large eggs

¾ cup plus 1 tablespoon sugar
½ teaspoon vanilla bean paste or
  vanilla extract
1 heaping tablespoon aniseeds

Preheat the oven to 350°. Whisk together the flour, baking powder, and baking soda in a medium bowl and set aside. Beat together the eggs, sugar, and vanilla bean paste in the bowl of a standing mixer with the whisk attachment on medium speed until thick and pale yellow (it should fall from the whisk in a wide ribbon), 8–10 minutes.

Remove the bowl from the mixer. Fold the flour mixture into the egg mixture in three batches with a rubber spatula, folding after each addition until just combined. Fold in the aniseeds. The dough will be very sticky.

Line two baking sheets with parchment paper. Using floured hands, shape the dough into four 5 × 2-inch logs on the baking sheets. Leave at least 2 inches between the logs; the dough will rise considerably as it bakes.

Bake until the logs are pale golden brown, about 20 minutes, rotating the baking sheets halfway through. Remove the logs from the oven and let them cool on the baking sheets for a few minutes. Reduce the oven temperature to 300°.

Using a serrated knife, cut the warm logs crosswise into ½-inch-thick biscotti. Place them cut side up in a single layer on the baking sheets. Bake for 5 minutes, then turn them over and bake until pale golden brown, about 5 minutes. Remove the biscotti from the oven and transfer them to wire racks to cool completely. They will keep in an airtight container for up to 2 weeks.

Overleaf, left page: Almond "Cookie" Tart; right page, top to bottom: Almond Cookies, Zaletti, and Biscotti di Anice

ZALETTI
makes about 40 cookies

We like to use medium stone-ground cornmeal for these currant-studded cookies. If you prefer a finer crunch, you can use finely ground cornmeal. This versatile dough can also be rolled out with a rolling pin and cut into small, dainty circles.

1 cup dried currants
¼ cup dark rum
1 cup plus 2 tablespoons stone-ground cornmeal
1¼ cups all-purpose flour, plus more for dusting
½ teaspoon baking soda

½ teaspoon baking powder
½ teaspoon salt
4 large egg yolks
½ cup sugar
6 tablespoons melted, unsalted butter, cooled
Finely grated zest of 2 lemons

Preheat the oven to 350°. Soak the currants in the rum in a small bowl until plump. Meanwhile, whisk together the cornmeal, flour, baking soda, baking powder, and salt in a medium mixing bowl and set aside.

Beat the egg yolks in the bowl of a standing mixer with the paddle attachment on medium speed. Gradually add the sugar, beating until thick and pale yellow. Beat in the melted butter and lemon zest, beating until smooth. Gradually add the cornmeal mixture, beating until well combined. The dough should be firm; if it is too dry, beat in some of the rum from the currants, 1 tablespoon at time, to soften it. Remove the bowl from the mixer. Drain the currants completely and stir them into the dough.

Lightly flour a work surface. Divide the dough in half and shape each half into two 2-inch square logs about 10 inches long. Brush off any excess flour from the logs, then cut them into ½-inch-thick pieces. Gently press each cookie into a diamond shape.

Line the baking sheets with parchment paper. Arrange the cookies on the sheets and bake until golden and crisp, 15–20 minutes. Remove the cookies from the oven and when cool enough to handle, peel them off the paper and transfer to a wire rack to cool completely. They will keep in an airtight container for up to 2 weeks.

Come visit us at thecanalhouse.com.